THE TEUTONIC KNIGHTS

Covering one of the most fascinating yet misunderstood periods in history, the MEDIEVAL LIVES series presents medieval people, concepts and events, drawing on political and social history, philosophy, material culture (art, architecture and archaeology) and the history of science. These books are global and wide-ranging in scope, encompassing both Western and non-Western subjects, and span the fifth to the fifteenth centuries, tracing significant developments from the collapse of the Roman Empire onwards.

SERIES EDITOR: Deirdre Jackson

THE TEUTONIC KNIGHTS

Rise and Fall of a Religious Corporation

ALEKSANDER PLUSKOWSKI

REAKTION BOOKS

*To my mother, Irena, who sparked my interest
in the Teutonic Knights all those years ago*

Published by Reaktion Books Ltd
Unit 32, Waterside
44–48 Wharf Road
London N1 7UX, UK
www.reaktionbooks.co.uk

First published 2024
Copyright © Aleksander Pluskowski 2024

Printed and bound in India by Replika Press Pvt. Ltd

A catalogue record for this book is available from the British Library

ISBN 978 1 78914 868 8

CONTENTS

Introduction

The Teutonic Order, also known as the Teutonic Knights, was the last of the great military orders to be founded in the Holy Land in the twelfth century. It would become one of the most powerful religious institutions in medieval Christendom, and leave a profound legacy that continues to resonate into the present day. This book provides a short introduction to the Order, tracking its development from a field hospital established outside the walls of Acre during the Third Crusade through to its meteoric rise in northeastern Europe as a major territorial ruler. The Order came to dominate the crusades that transformed the pagan tribal lands of the eastern Baltic into the Catholic polities of Prussia and Livonia. Here, the Order built a unique set of fortified convents, including the largest castle in Christendom as its headquarters. This book concludes with the Order's eventual decline over the course of the fifteenth century, following a disastrous war with Poland-Lithuania, and the transformative impact of the Reformation that secularized its Prussian branch and eventually, in the face of military defeat, its Livonian branch. This ended three centuries of theocratic rule by one of the most remarkable religious corporations in the history of Europe. The Order would continue in the Holy Roman Empire as a religious and charitable organization, but its role as a military force and its involvement with crusading had come to an end.

A Note on Names and Abbreviations

Throughout this book, names have been anglicized where possible for the sake of consistency. At the first mention of a major historical place name in each chapter, the modern name is included in parentheses. Where recent archaeological excavations or museums are referred to, the modern site name is used. Abbreviations are used as follows:

Est. = Estonian
Ger. = German
Lat. = Latin
Latv. = Latvian
Lit. = Lithuanian
Pol. = Polish

ONE

The German Hospital of the Third Crusade: The Origins of the Teutonic Order

On 27 November 1095, in response to a plea from the Byzantine emperor, the leader of the Eastern Roman Empire, the pope called for a holy war to aid eastern Christians against the Seljuk Turks and to take control of Jerusalem from its Muslim rulers. Christians considered the city to be the most sacred place in the world – the site of Christ's passion, burial and resurrection. Those who 'took the cross' and embarked on what was essentially an armed pilgrimage would have all their sins forgiven. If they died on the way or in battle, their soul's entry to heaven was guaranteed. The campaign to reclaim Jerusalem, later called 'The First Crusade', began with 'The People's Crusade', a spontaneous mass migration largely of peasants, which ended when most of its participants were massacred in Anatolia in October 1096. Following in their wake, a series of armies led by some of the most prominent nobles of Western Europe gathered at Constantinople and fought their way south to Jerusalem. This was a difficult and dangerous journey that took two years and saw the crusading host reduced to a fraction of its original size. Against all the odds, they captured Jerusalem on 15 July 1099.[1] During this time and in the years that followed, crusading lords carved out four territories in the Levant, which became known as Outremer. These Catholic principalities, the largest of which was the Kingdom of Jerusalem, have also been called 'crusader states' by historians.[2] The seizure

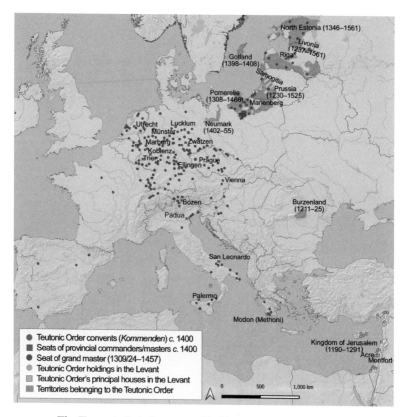

The Teutonic Order's territorial holdings, 1190–1561.

of Jerusalem transformed crusading into a widespread movement in Catholic Europe.

The Military Orders

The formation of the military orders over the course of the twelfth century saw the creation of permanent religious institutions that became wholly dedicated to the crusading movement and the defence of Christendom, initially in the Levant and not long after also in Iberia. The Templars, Hospitallers and finally the Teutonic Order would become powerful international corporations, accumulating vast estates in the Levantine crusader states as well as within Europe. The Templars had been formed by a group of knights who remained in Jerusalem after the First Crusade, and became attached to the Holy Sepulchre under the supervision of its prior, the Patriarch. In 1120 some of them decided to break away from the Holy Sepulchre and establish a separate group, with the aim of providing security for growing numbers of pilgrims making their way to the Holy Land. The first crusader king of Jerusalem, Baldwin, granted them the buildings of the Al-Aqsa mosque on the Temple Mount, which had been repurposed as a royal palace after the city was taken in 1099. This was believed to be the Temple of Solomon. From this, they adopted the name the Poor Knights of Christ and the Temple of Solomon in Jerusalem, shortened to Templars. By the time they were formally recognized by the pope as a religious order in 1129 and given a primitive rule under the guidance of the Cistercians, the Templars had a clear mission statement: to protect pilgrims and holy places. Thanks to their promotion by the influential Cistercian abbot and orator Bernard of Clairvaux as the 'new knighthood' of Christendom, they rapidly accumulated charitable donations of land and privileges.

The Hospitallers or Order of the Brothers of the Hospital of St John of Jerusalem were formed from an earlier Amalfitan hospice that had survived the siege of 1099, and would come to play a major role in the revival of pilgrimage and the resettlement of the city in the early decades of the twelfth century. The hospice then came under the authority of the newly established Augustinian Canons of the Holy Sepulchre. It quickly attracted royal patronage from the new dynasty of Jerusalem's monarchs and in 1112 it was granted exemption from paying tithes by the city's patriarch. The following year the hospital was recognized as an autonomous religious order by the pope and over the coming decades received various privileges. Like the

Templars, the Hospitallers would answer to the pope alone as their ecclesiastical overlord, although in reality they were able to operate independently. The order also became increasingly involved in military activities in the latter half of the twelfth century, being given the responsibility of garrisoning castles and defending territory in the crusader states. Both the Templars and Hospitallers raised money through alms-collection, grants of lands and privileges in the Levant and Europe. They grew in wealth, size and military strength, and largely recruited in Western Europe. They managed their resources through a hierarchical system of commanderies or preceptories, which were grouped under provinces or priories.

Despite decades of growth, the Battle of Cresson on 1 May 1187 and the more disastrous Battle of Hattin on 4 July had a profound impact on the miliary orders. Both the Templars and Hospitallers lost the majority of their Levantine knights and leadership, although the Templar master survived. Within a few months, Saladin's army had captured more than fifty towns, including the port of Acre, and on 2 October Jerusalem itself had surrendered. The Templars and Hospitallers lost substantial properties and lands, including their headquarters, as the Kingdom of Jerusalem contracted. These events would prompt calls for another crusade to recover the holy city, one which would see the rise of a new military order.

The Third Crusade

Pope Gregory VIII's call for a new crusade had been prompted by the news from Hattin, and was further energized by the loss of Jerusalem. Kings and nobles responded enthusiastically from across the Angevin Empire, Capetian France, the Holy Roman Empire, Hungary and Sicily.[3] The Second Crusade in 1147, a response to the sacking of Edessa, had seen extensive participation from German contingents, with southerners joining the German king Conrad III's campaign in the Levant and northerners targeting the pagan Wends. This time the German crusading effort was led by Emperor Frederick Barbarossa, who had participated in his uncle Conrad III's campaign four decades earlier.[4] On 27 March 1188 Frederick called an assembly at Mainz, which he referred to as the *Curia Christi* (Court of Christ). Here he publicly took the cross, along with his son Frederick of Swabia and a number of German nobles, knights and bishops. He then gave instructions for mustering an army at Regensburg to assemble the following year on 23 April, on the feast day of the most important crusader saint, St George. In the end, the emperor's crusading host was delayed, but one contingent did manage to set off in April 1189: a fleet of fifty ships carrying around 12,000 men recruited from the cities of Bremen and Lübeck. They arrived in Acre in September and joined Guy of Lusignan's siege of the city. Guy still claimed the title of King of Jerusalem, although his authority was entirely dependent on his wife Queen Sibylla.

The emperor had finally set off on 11 May, and others joined his army as it proceeded along the Danube and across Bulgaria towards Constantinople. Frederick then made it as far as Cilicia, but while crossing the Saleph river on 10 June 1190, his horse slipped and he fell into the water and drowned. A large part of the imperial army returned, but his son continued with 5,000 men and eventually reached Acre in October. A few months later, during the course of the siege, Frederick of Swabia succumbed to dysentery and died, and Leopold V of Austria assumed command of the imperial force. The arrival of the armies of Philip of France in April and Richard I of England in June quickly brought the siege to an end and the garrison surrendered on 12 July. Philip then returned to France, while Richard tried unsuccessfully to capture Jerusalem. His failure has contributed to negative appraisals of the Third Crusade; however, the

Christian victories along the Levantine coast managed to secure
the remnants of the crusader states for another hundred years.[5]

The Foundation of the German Hospital

When the contingent from Bremen and Lübeck arrived, the siege
of Acre was already well underway.[6] The Germans quickly established a small field hospital outside the city walls, consisting of
a tent allegedly made from a ship's sail. The hospital took the
form of a lay brotherhood run by a master (Lat. *magister*), similar
to those found in the empire, and the brethren provided care for
the wounded and ill, as well as burial for the dead.[7] Soon after,
Guy of Lusignan promised the newly established hospital the
property of the former Armenian hospice within Acre. The hospital began to cater to the needs of the large numbers of German
crusaders, who clearly needed to be able to communicate with
those caring for them. Indeed, the construction of a German
pilgrim hospital in June 1191 in Brindisi, southern Italy, was also
probably a response to the substantial numbers of German crusaders travelling along the central Mediterranean route to the
Levant. One of those treated in the German hospital at Acre was
the emperor's son, Frederick of Swabia. As he lay dying in January
1191, he asked for the hospital to take responsibility for his burial,
a request which the Hospitallers allegedly contested, as they
claimed a monopoly over all burial (and profits deriving from
this) in Acre. Frederick also wrote to his brother, Henry VI, the
new emperor, asking him to confirm the hospital's foundation
and to obtain papal recognition for the fledging institution.

After the surrender of Acre, the German hospital was granted
buildings within the city, close to the gate of St Nicholas, by Guy,
who was still clinging onto the crown of Jerusalem. This became
the centre of the German quarter and eventually included a
castle and tower. The hospital then continued serving pilgrims

coming into Acre. This initial complex of buildings expanded in size over time, as royal support for the brethren steadily continued. By February of the following year, the Hospitallers had recognized the German hospital and their master granted land in Acre to a brother (Lat. *frater*) who was described as the Master of the Hospital of the Germans in Acre. Emperor Henry vi became a keen supporter of the German hospital, granting it properties and trading privileges in southern Italy, the first of many estates that enabled the brethren to channel resources from Europe to the Levant.

In 1196 the pope had recognized the Acre hospital as composed of regular brothers (Lat. *fratres*), with the name *hospitalis Sancta Maria Alamannorum Ierosolimitanum* (Hospital of St Mary of the Germans in Jerusalem). The choice to connect the new hospital's title to Jerusalem, as justified by a member of the Order writing decades later, was motivated by the hope that the Order's principal house would eventually be established in the holy city once it had come back under Christian rule. A hospital and church called St Mary of the Germans had existed in Jerusalem from 1118, under the authority of the Hospitallers. Some of its members may even have stayed on after Jerusalem was taken by Saladin in 1187, while others fled back to German lands. Later the Teutonic Order would attempt to link its origins to the Jerusalem hospital, in a mythologizing attempt to demonstrate continuity and to elevate its reputation.[8] The name *Ordinis Theutonici* began to be used to refer to the Acre hospital in the thirteenth century. The word *Teutonicus*, deriving from Classical Latin, was used by medieval authors as a synonym for German people and language, and from the sixteenth century *Ordinis Theutonici* was directly translated into English as 'Teutonic Order', a name that, despite its archaism, remains widely used in Anglophone literature today. The name 'Teutonic Knights' was applied much later, appearing in English from the sixteenth century, but it has been used for the title of this book to denote the medieval Teutonic Order, whose military role essentially ended with the secularization of its Prussian and Livonian branches.

Militarization

In 1195 Emperor Henry VI launched his crusade to the Holy Land with the intention of completing the original objective of the Third Crusade – the retaking of Jerusalem. Henry's army arrived at Acre late in September 1197, but he did not accompany them and died in Messina. Although the crusaders had begun to lay siege to the castle of Toron, Henry's death prompted them to withdraw and abandon their efforts. In March 1198 the leaders of the German crusaders, including Frederick I, Duke of Austria, called for the German hospital to be militarized to bolster their attempt to recover Jerusalem. This proposal was approved by Aimery of Lusignan, the ruler of the remnant kingdom of Jerusalem and Cyprus, as well as by the local nobility. The hospital was given the rule of the Templars to structure its military organization, and the rule of the Hospitallers to govern its care for the infirm and poor. This completely transformed the institution, with the introduction of three vows that all brethren had to swear to abide by: obedience to the rule, celibacy and poverty. However, it appears the Hospitallers were intent on incorporating the German brethren into their ranks who, in response, turned to the Templars and placed themselves under their authority. In recognition of this, they were permitted to use the symbol of a 'wheel' (a circle) with a black half cross, alongside the Templars' characteristic white mantles.

The German hospital's new status was conferred in a ceremony in the Templars' palace in Acre and the first master, a Templar brother, was appointed: Henry Walpot of Bassenheim.

In a ceremonial gesture that marked the birth of the new military order, the Templar master handed over a copy of his order's rule and knighted the first *miles* (knight) of the Teutonic Order. The following year, Pope Innocent III confirmed the brethren's new role, extending their vocation to the waging of holy war against the enemies of Christendom. Moreover, the desire to retake

Depiction of the German *Minnesänger* (lyric poet) Tannhäuser dressed as a member of the Teutonic Order, from the *Codex Manesse*, c. 1300–40.

Jerusalem, which had motivated the crusades in the last decade
of the twelfth century, had a profound and lasting impact on the
Teutonic Order's identity, as expressed in its later statutes. However, by 1210 there appears to have been a deterioration in
relations between the German brethren and the Templars. The
latter had complained to the papacy that the Order's brethren
were wearing white mantles without their permission, suggest-
ing they had broken away from the Templars' authority and were
perceived to be acting too independently. Although the pope
nominally forbade the Order to use white mantles, by the time
of the Fifth Crusade (1217–21), they had adopted them along
with the black cross that would famously come to define their
emblem.

By this time, support for the Teutonic Order was flourishing.
The kings of Jerusalem continued to be generous with donations of privileges and property. Henry of Champagne gave the
Order a house in Jaffa and vineyards, as well as entrusting them
with the defence of a section of the walls of Acre. In 1198 King
Aimery provided the Order with an allowance of sugar to support
the infirmary, as well as a source of income and some pasture. In
1200 Bohemond III, the Prince of Antioch, granted the Order
trading rights in his principality, and they received support from
patrons in Armenian Cilicia. But the growing involvement of
German knights in crusading also represented a major stimulus
for the brethren. In exchange for providing hospital care as well
as aftercare for the soul, the Order received numerous gifts from
grateful benefactors, which included donations of land in Europe.
Some became lifelong benefactors. Others were moved to give
donations to the Order's houses within the empire or France. As
a result, the Order gradually developed financial independence
and started making purchases of land and property. This, in turn,
solidified their presence in the Holy Land and provided a steady
stream of income.

The Order's most enthusiastic supporters were the Hohen-staufen emperors, who saw themselves as defenders of the Holy Land and were keen to expand their influence over Christian territories in the Levant; both Cyprus and Armenia had become imperial vassals. While the Order was consistently supported by the imperial family and leading magnates like the dukes of Austria, there is no evidence it operated as a vassal or a tool of imperial politics. In fact, the Order remained politically neutral, performing a careful balancing act between its loyalty to both the emperor and pope, who were frequently rivals at this time. The Order remained dependent on the goodwill of both. The pope could dissolve the Order and strip the brethren of their special status. The emperor, in turn, could revoke any trading and taxation privileges that had been granted and take back their lands within his realm, depriving the Order of a major source of revenue. In the end, the Order was able to navigate this dangerous course through the volatile sea of international politics thanks to its astute and skilful leaders, in particular its fourth master, Herman of Salza, who held the post from 1210 to 1239. A *ministerialis* (or lesser noble) hailing from Thuringia who developed close ties to Emperor Frederick II, Salza would transform the Order from a small Levantine military order into an international political force.

TWO

Expansion and Loss in the Thirteenth Century: The Teutonic Order in the Holy Land

The thirteenth century was a formative period for the Teutonic Order. With papal and imperial support, it quickly developed into an independent and wealthy institution. Successive popes had reaffirmed the brethren's exemption from all jurisdictions, save that of the Holy See. In 1223 Honorius III permitted the brethren to remit sins in exchange for alms. Adopting the statutes of the Templars and Hospitallers, the Order gradually modified these to fit its own needs. The Hospitallers had laid claim to authority over the Order, arguing the institution was ultimately derived from the earlier German hospital in Jerusalem, which had been founded in 1118. The Order, in turn, denied this connection (when inconvenient) and worked hard to ensure its independent status. Involvement in the Baltic crusading frontier contributed to this and by 1236 the brethren were considered a suitable model for new military orders, as the pope confirmed the militarization of the (short-lived) English Order of St Thomas of Acre to follow the Teutonic Order's rule. In 1244 the pope permitted the brethren to remove any clauses in their statutes they considered redundant, essentially confirming their autonomy. Charitable donations from the Hohenstaufens, imperial magnates and German pilgrims, as well as Outremer's kings and nobility, enabled the Order to build up its estates and financial independence in both the Levant and Europe. Its ranks also began to swell with recruits. In 1210 there may have been as few as ten brother-knights (Lat. *milites*), but when the brethren's forces participated in the battle of La Forbie in 1244, some four hundred men, most likely a combination of brother-knights, turcopoles (light cavalry used within Byzantine armies for skirmishing) and lay brothers (Lat. *confratres*; affiliates who did not take the Order's vows), are documented. Half-sisters (Lat. *consorores*, Ger. *Halpswesteren*) are also noted.[1]

From its earliest years the Order was a transnational institution, with holdings in southern Italy, Sicily, Cyprus and Cilicia, alongside those in Outremer.[2] Soon it would also acquire estates in Bohemia and other parts of the Holy Roman Empire.[3] Under the leadership of Herman of Salza, the Order became committed to defending multiple frontiers of Christendom. From 1211 the brethren became involved in the defence of the eastern frontier of the Hungarian kingdom, in 1218 they joined the flotilla of the Fifth Crusade to Egypt and from 1225 Salza entered into negotiations with Konrad, Duke of Mazovia, which led to crusades against the Prussian tribes, joining the ongoing war in adjacent Livonia a decade later. In these years the brethren developed a reputation as an effective fighting force and were celebrated in epic works. The Order's involvement in these various campaigns eventually reshaped the organization's character and purpose, enabling it to endure after the loss of Acre in 1291. In the early decades of the thirteenth century, the Order's masters sought to reconcile their rival patrons, the emperor and the pope, but as more resources were invested in Prussia and Livonia, tensions also surfaced between the Order's higher officials. Until it became clear that the Holy Land was a lost cause, the Order's masters were able to ensure the principal focus remained on the Levant. After Salza's death, subsequent masters were more inclined to take sides, provoking at times the emperor and at other times

the pope, a political tug of war that ended with the death of
Frederick II in 1250.

Herman of Salza and the Fifth Crusade

The Order's rapid development in the early thirteenth century
was largely thanks to the leadership of its fourth master, Herman
of Salza, who reigned from about 1210 to 1239. These were
formative years for the Order, and Salza was a highly skilled
and tactful politician who maintained the difficult position of
neutrality in his loyalty to both Emperor Frederick II and the
pope. As one historian has written, throughout his career Salza
acted as the 'servant of two masters', as both a papal and imperial
emissary.[4] Hailing from a Thuringian family of minor nobles, he
arrived in the Holy Land with Landgrave Herman I in 1196.
The connection with Thuringia remained strong, and the Order
was granted various privileges and property in the principality,
while its noble families sent their sons to join its ranks. Salza was
able to secure the support of competing imperial factions, including the Welf family, which contended with the Hohenstaufens
for the imperial throne, and notably the Order did not take sides
in the imperial civil war that raged throughout the early decades
of the thirteenth century. Salza was also able to secure Armenian
patronage and in 1212 accompanied an imperial emissary to
bestow a crown upon the new king, Leon, in recognition of
his loyalty to the empire. In turn, the Order was granted the
castle of Amudain, and would remain a beneficiary of Armenian
patronage. The Order constructed a new keep at Amudain, similar to the principal towers at Montfort and Jiddin, and even
comparable to fortifications in the empire.[5]

Pope Innocent had proclaimed the Fifth Crusade in 1213, but
died before the campaign began. Honorius III continued the call
for a crusade and in the summer of 1217 tens of thousands of

soldiers mustered at Acre, many coming from the Holy Roman Empire. This provided Salza with the opportunity to showcase the Order's commitment to the recovery of Jerusalem. He participated in the council of crusading leaders and the Order's brethren also contributed to the construction of the Templar castle at Atlit. In May 1218 the crusaders, along with the Order's forces, sailed for Egypt and laid siege to Damietta, which fell on 5 November 1219. Here, the brethren distinguished themselves during a series of assaults and in the defence of the crusading army's camp, taking heavy casualties in the process. Salza was regularly involved in the war councils and supported the decision to advance towards Cairo. He also travelled to the West to keep the pope and emperor updated of the events of the campaign. The army remained in Damietta until the arrival of Duke Louis of Bavaria in the spring of 1221, then finally marched south along the Nile towards Cairo. Here, the campaign floundered as the Nile flooded, and the crusaders finally surrendered in August 1221. Their leaders were offered up as hostages to secure a truce and the city of Damietta was returned to the Egyptian sultan. Salza played an important role in the negotiations, reflecting his importance and value. He was delegated to surrender Damietta, along with the Templar master, and was also offered up as a hostage together with the leaders of the other two great military orders.

Despite the failure of the Fifth Crusade, the Teutonic Order's reputation was significantly enhanced, especially among German crusaders. There was an influx of donations from pilgrims and nobles, and several crusaders were moved to join the Order as brothers, a recruitment drive supported by the pope. This enabled the Order to bolster its membership by recruiting trained knights who wished to remain in the Holy Land to continue the fight for Jerusalem, especially in the light of the Fifth Crusade's failures. Many others became lay brothers of the Order. Large numbers of lay brothers became involved in the Fifth Crusade, and the pope permitted their burial in the Holy Land by the Order's brethren. Indeed, in 1223, the pope encouraged crusaders to become lay brothers in exchange for the remission of a seventh of their penance. Seven years later, the pope offered the same incentive to those who contributed to the building of the Order's castle of Montfort. The number of papal privileges conferred on the Order substantially increased, although some have argued this was largely due to the influence of Emperor Frederick II. This series of charters included exemption from the payment of tithes, and the same privileges as granted to the Templars and Hospitallers, essentially elevating the Teutonic Order to the same status. The Order's finances were further protected from ecclesiastical tithes and other financial burdens imposed by the Church. Following the campaign, Frederick also gave the Order various benefits, including income from a number of ports in southern Italy and Sicily, as well as granting the brethren more land.

Frederick then began preparing for another crusade and Salza became closely involved in the recruitment drive for this campaign. He was also involved in diplomatic efforts to settle disputes between the emperor and his vassals in Italy, and orchestrated a treaty with the Danish king Valdemar concerning the frontier territories of Schleswig and Holstein. On the emperor's instructions, he travelled to Frankfurt in the spring of 1224, where he made a speech to the German nobles encouraging them to participate in the new crusade, although his efforts were largely unsuccessful. Two years later he was ordered by the pope to conduct another recruitment drive and this time was able to persuade the Landgrave of Thuringia and seven hundred knights to join the crusade. The Order provided ships for the enterprise, built in such a way as to enable mounted knights to be directly deployed into battle, in the manner of an amphibious assault.

Salza was even involved in mediating Frederick's marriage to Isabella, the daughter of John of Brienne, the king of Jerusalem.

She was later escorted by a brother of the Order from Acre to Italy for the second enactment of the marriage ceremony, this time with Frederick in attendance. As it turned out, whether in collusion with Salza or not, Frederick promptly seized the crown of Jerusalem. Moreover, since he failed in his oath to go on crusade, he was excommunicated. This finally galvanized him into action, and the emperor's campaign was again supported by the Order – somewhat awkwardly given that the crusade was led by someone who had been officially cast out by the Church, with the danger of offending the pope. The Order contributed to repairing Jaffa's defences and Salza acted as an imperial emissary to the Egyptian sultan. Frederick would be crowned in the Holy Sepulchre on 18 March 1229, following a treaty with the sultan to return Jerusalem, Bethlehem and Nazareth to Christian control. Although Salza had dissuaded Frederick from receiving Mass in the Holy Sepulchre, the emperor's coronation, without papal endorsement, prompted the Archbishop of Caesarea to place the whole of Jerusalem under interdict. Salza had been asked to translate the emperor's speech in which he declared his views of the papacy, an action that prompted rebuke from Patriarch Gerold of Jerusalem, and from Pope Gregory IX. Fighting broke out between Frederick's and Gerold's men in Acre. As a result, in August 1229 the pope placed the Teutonic Order under the authority of the Hospitallers, and asked Gerold to enforce this. However, Salza, the consummate diplomat, soon restored friendly relations with his ecclesiastical sovereign and within a few months the Order's independent status was restored.

Frederick thanked the Order by permitting them to fortify Montfort and granting them the buildings of the former German hospital in Jerusalem, as well as a royal palace on the Armenian route and further trading privileges. In the meantime, the deposed king of Jerusalem, John of Brienne, would himself lead the papal army against Frederick's domain, but his efforts largely failed and ultimately, he would be driven from Rome. Salza, representing the emperor, attended the peace negotiations at San Germano, which were concluded on 23 July 1230. Yet within a decade the peace had been shattered by a conflict between the emperor, his son and the Lombard communes, which threatened the pope's authority in northern Italy. When imperial forces finally invaded Sardinia, the pope excommunicated Frederick again, having earlier excommunicated his son. Throughout this period Salza continued to act as a mediator between the warring factions.

Military Organization

The retaking of Jerusalem and the Holy Land for Christendom became the Teutonic Order's defining *raison d'être*, and following its militarization the brethren began to compare themselves to the Maccabees of the Old Testament. This famed group of Jewish fighters had rebelled against the Hellenistic Seleucid Empire and, with small numbers facing overwhelming odds, taken back Jerusalem. The papal bull *Audita Tremendi*, which had been issued by Pope Gregory in October 1187 to rally support for the retaking of Jerusalem, had directly referred to the Maccabees as the exemplary model of martyrdom for crusaders to follow. The Order soon became recognized as the new Maccabees – the new defenders of the Holy Land – by its supporters and the papacy, and alluded to them in the prologue of its later statutes. The Order's organization in the early decades of the thirteenth century reflected this developing military role.[6]

Overall governance was the responsibility of the master, an office later differentiated from the provincial land masters who were responsible for territories beyond the Levant. By the mid-thirteenth century this led to the adoption of the overarching title grand master (Lat. *magister generalis*; Ger. *Hochmeister*).

While the first master of the Teutonic Order was selected by the Templars, later ones were appointed by the officers of the Order representing all of its provinces who came together in a chapter. On 14 September every year a general chapter was organized to discuss the Order's business and various appointments. During this assembly, every office, except for that of the master, would either be reconfirmed or handed over to another individual. The commanders (Lat. *commendator*; Ger. *Komtur*) of Cyprus and Armenia were expected to be present, while attendance for other provincial leaders was optional. This is because in principle the general chapter was to be held in Outremer, but in practice its location varied, and several took place within the empire.

Masters were expected to have military experience and religious devotion and were typically officials who had already held a variety of roles within the Order. However, there was also a political dimension to their appointments as the chapter was obliged to elect someone who was acceptable to the entire organization. On the battlefield the master led the Order's army and was supplied with an escort of turcopoles and brother-knights, as well as non-military personnel.

The next most important office was the marshal, first mentioned in 1208 and a position adopted from the Templars. He was responsible for all military matters, including personnel and equipment. On the battlefield the marshal commanded the Order's army if the master was absent and was given an escort of two brother-knights and two turcopoles, who were charged with protecting the army's standard. Marshals were also appointed early on in Livonia and Prussia, given the necessity for military organization in those provinces. The other high offices included the grand commander, who dealt with shipping, provisioning, the Order's treasury, general administration and also had a military role, deputizing for the marshal. Since the grand master often spent more time outside Outremer, the grand

commander would often act as his deputy in dealing with the general business of the Order.

The grand commander's deputy was the vice-commander, first mentioned in 1230 as the minor preceptor, and he was also supported by the treasurer. The quartermaster was in charge of all clothing and armour for the brethren, while lesser offices included the turcopolier, a military role also adopted from the Templars, the saddler and a brother in charge of the smithy. Finally, there were officials who managed the Order's territories outside Outremer, positions which developed out of necessity as the brethren expanded their holdings: the masters of Prussia, Livonia and Germany (the empire), and the commanders of Austria, Apulia, Achaea and Armenia. They managed the military and financial resources for their territories and were responsible for providing supplies from their estates. In comparison to the other military orders, these provincial commanders were more on an equal footing with the grand master, in particular the masters of Prussia and Livonia.

Each of the Order's convents was supposed to house twelve brother-knights, who could field up to four horses and were supported by an esquire. These brethren largely came from aristocratic backgrounds, although this requirement was only enforced from the end of the thirteenth century. Brother-sergeants (Lat. *servientes*, also known as Ger. *Graumäntler* or 'grey mantles') who provided light armoured cavalry were recruited from families of burghers (town dwellers) and rural gentry. The Order's statutes, like those of the Templars and Hospitallers, specified how the brethren should conduct themselves in battle. The importance of formation and discipline was emphasized; brother-knights were expected to remain silent and were not permitted

Conrad of Thuringia's funerary effigy in St Elizabeth's Church, Marburg, Germany. Conrad succeeded Herman of Salza as master of the Teutonic Order in 1239, but reigned for little over a year.

to ride ahead of the standard bearer. Embracing the outward appearance of austerity like the Templars, the Order's brethren were expected to forsake luxury and excessively decorated armour and equestrian equipment.

Following its militarization, the Order's principal military commitment in the eastern Mediterranean was during the Fifth Crusade, after which the treaty with the Sultan of Egypt in 1229 reduced the burden of defensive responsibilities for the brethren in the Holy Land. In 1230 the Order would begin its crusades against the pagan Prussian tribes and from then its involvement in the Baltic would grow exponentially (see Chapter Four). The brethren did not involve themselves in the so-called Ibelin-Lombard war of 1230–39 between the Ibelins (one of the most powerful noble families in the crusader states) and Frederick's officials in the Levant. However, continuing to play the role of masterful diplomats, they received lands and privileges from both the imperial and Ibelin factions; in Acre, a power centre for the Ibelins, the Order's assets continued to grow. But they were now committing increasingly more resources to the eastern Baltic. In May 1237, following the Order's absorption of the Sword Brothers, the brethren also became committed to territorial rule and further conquests in Livonia. This prompted the reallocation of resources, and Ludwig of Öttingen took sixty brother-knights to the Baltic, representing a significant military commitment to this new theatre of crusading. This had a wider effect too, as it redirected German (and other North European) crusaders away from the Levant. To manage its growing territorial assets in the conquered tribal lands, the brethren also established new provincial headquarters and Herman Balk, the Order's German master, was elected master of the Order's territory in Prussia from the onset of the crusade in 1230, and subsequently as master of Livonia for a short time from 1237 until his death the following year, when he was replaced by

Dietrich of Grüningen, who would also later hold the office of Prussian master.

Despite increasing commitments in the eastern Baltic, the Order's leading officials continued to view themselves as members of a Levantine organization. The earliest version of the Order's statutes dates to 1264, consisting of the rule, laws and customs, with a number of subsidiary sections: the prologue, vigils, calendar, Easter tables and genuflections.[7] By this time the Order was governing large swathes of territory in Prussia and Livonia, and this document clearly accommodated the Order's involvement in different frontiers, such as permitting the use of specific weapons in particular regions. However, its organizational structure in Outremer was emphasized throughout. This was to be the master's residence, the location for the general chapter and for the master's election. Livonia and Prussia are mentioned on only three occasions, while Armenia is mentioned four times. Given the statutes were written by the Levantine chapter this is perhaps unsurprising. With the consolidation of its holdings in the Levant and the expansion of its domains in the eastern Baltic, the Order's officials were increasingly required to serve as territorial administrators.

Territorial Administration

In the decades following its militarization, the Teutonic Order would actively support German crusaders who came to the Holy Land with the aim of retaking Jerusalem. These crusaders would repay the Order with grants of land and property. This resulted in the incremental acquisition of vast estates across large swathes of imperial territories. This, in turn, provided an increasing amount of revenue, as well as supplies for the Order's hospitals and military installations in the Levant. Leopold vi, Duke of Austria, was a major patron of the Order in its formative years. He granted them property in his realm, and during the course of the Fifth Crusade donated the sum of 6,000 marks to the brethren, which provided the bulk of the money needed to purchase their first estate within the Kingdom of Jerusalem.

In 1220 the Order bought the lands of Joscelin III, Count of Edessa, from his son-in-law Otto, Count of Henneburg. Otto was leaving the Holy Land together with his family. He had lost much of his land to the Muslims, and the only castle the Order obtained through this purchase was Castellum Regis. This, together with the acquisition of nearby Montfort eight years later, saw the Order develop their principal power base in the foothills of the western Galilee, northeast of Acre. Here they accumulated numerous grants of lands, many of which were donations and others they purchased. They may have found it easier to acquire properties here as a number were damaged or destroyed by a severe earthquake that had hit the Acre region in 1202.[8] For the villages on these lands, the Order acted as overlord and wielded secular authority, but the brethren's main interests lay in the productive value of their Galilee estates, which supplied oil, wine and sugar, as well as cereals. They also owned a number of mills. In addition to the two castles at the centre of the Joscelin estate, the Order built the castle of Jiddin (or Judin) after 1220, on a ridge overlooking the Wadi Jiddin. This would be lost by 1271.[9] Jiddin was situated on the road between Castellum Regis and Acre, which represented a vital communication supply route connecting the Order's two principal houses.

Acre

In Acre the Order owned a complex in the eastern part of the city that included a tower, described by the Templar of Tyre as large and beautiful as that of the Templar palace. On maps of the thirteenth-century city this is referred to as *Turris Alamanorum*.

This remained the Order's headquarters until 1291, with some functions transferred to Montfort castle. The Order was also given part of the town defences to maintain. In 1193 Henry II granted the Order a barbican at the gate of St Nicholas, along with towers, walls, a moat and a vault in the town wall, a section of the forewall extending from the gate. Parts of this may have been uncovered by a series of excavations in the twentieth century, which included substantial public and private buildings, as well as industrial installations including a possible sugar refinery and workshops, which had been destroyed in 1291. The church in the German quarter, where Duke Frederick of Swabia was buried, has not been found, as the structure was burnt down by the Templars in 1242 during a period of unrest. After the loss of Montfort in 1271, the Order bought property in the northeast of Acre, with the result that the German quarter occupied a large part of this corner of the city up to the southern moat of the citadel.[10] The Order had a periodic, but important, source of income from the shipping and market taxes of Acre.

Montfort

The construction of Montfort castle (or Ger. Starkenberg, 'strong mountain') began in 1226 and finished sometime between 1239 and 1243. Crusaders from Frederick II's army contributed to the building works, as did Bohemond IV of Antioch; following a plea for help from Salza in March 1229, Gregory IX granted remission of one-seventh of penance to any pilgrims who helped with the castle's construction. The fortress was built on a mountainous spur where two valleys converged. Protected on three sides by steep slopes, the builders cut two deep moats at its eastern end, severing the castle from the rest of the spur. Here, the earliest part of the castle was constructed, a large tower that probably contained a chapel on its first floor, followed by a two-storey elongated building that extended over the spur to the west. This

Ruins of the Teutonic Order's castle at Montfort, north Israel.

may have housed the dormitory and refectory for the brethren, and at its eastern end was a kitchen and latrines. Beyond this, a three-storey building contained a large hall and most probably the domestic quarters of the Order's castellan (first documented from 1240), as well as a comfortable residence for the master. A further vaulted building was added beyond this, and a wall enclosed the whole complex, accessible through a three-storey gate tower. The complex was unusual for a military order insofar as it did not contain a courtyard, nor was there any attempt to organize the buildings along a claustral plan suitable for a monastic lifestyle. Instead, these spaces were accommodated within the confines of the elongated spur.

An outer wall was built on the north and west slopes, punctuated with two semicircular towers and four gates. It enclosed a ward used for a range of functions, including stables. At the base of the slope, a two-storey building was constructed with a mill in its lower level. The upper storey, consisting of a vaulted hall in the Gothic style with three bays, has been widely interpreted as a guesthouse, or potentially a dormitory for female pilgrims or sisters of the Order.[11] Despite the substantial investment in its construction, the castle was not in a strategically favourable location. Lacking suitable vantage points, it did not control any important roads and was far from the coast. The deliberate choice of this remote location for what became the Order's principal administrative centre (alongside Acre) has been interpreted in the context of the deteriorating relationships between the brethren and the other military orders, especially the Templars.[12]

The 'Great Hall' of the Teutonic Order's castle at Montfort, the exact function of which is unclear.

Holdings elsewhere

The other region in Outremer where the Order acquired land and property, albeit for a relatively shorter period of time, was the eastern part of the lordship of Sidon, which stretched between Beirut and Tyre. Following the Mongol attack on Sidon in 1260, both the Templars and the Teutonic Order purchased what remained of the lordship. The brethren also acquired the Cave of Tyron, a fortified outpost cut into a cliff overlooking the Beqa valley, although they only held it for a few years. The Order additionally held properties in several of the key towns of Outremer (Jaffa, Ramla, Gaza, Ascalon, Sidon and Tyre), and acquired two towers in Caesarea and three towers in Tripoli. As it gained more holdings, the Order's organization evolved to meet the demands of managing its growing estates. The grand commander became responsible for the administration of rural holdings, including pack animals and grain. He was located in Acre and supported by a number of local administrators. Again, the model for this was provided by the Templars and Hospitallers, but in comparison the Teutonic Order's properties and lands in the Levant were small in number.

In addition to its holdings within the heartlands of the Holy Roman Empire and, through ties between the Hohenstaufens and the Castilian court, in Iberia, the Order also acquired land in France, Italy, Sicily, Armenia and Greece, regions connected to the crusader states of the Levant. In Armenia the Order held the castles of Amudain and Harunia, as well as their associated estates, and in Cyprus they most probably had a hospital in Famagusta, dedicated to St Mary, along with some rural estates. The lands of the Order provided it with an income, both in terms of leasing and selling tradable goods. This would be supplemented with goods and revenue from its estates in Europe, which from the 1230s would also be sent to the eastern Baltic.

Goods destined for the Levant were shipped in from ports in Apulia and Sicily. Most of what was shipped to Acre was grain, as well as horses. The Order acquired various holdings around key ports such as Brindisi and Bari. These, in turn, provided an additional source of income, alongside the harbour tolls of Italian ports granted by Frederick II. The brethren were not required to pay taxes on their own cargo and in 1221 Frederick released the Order from all taxation requirements within the empire. Control over these supply lines depended on imperial favour, which is why the Order's leaders (and in particular Salza) invested so much time on diplomacy. As the Order lost much of its land in the Levant to the Mamluks, particularly in the 1270s, it became increasingly reliant on overseas provisioning.

Healthcare

The Teutonic Order began as a hospital, and this function remained an important part of the brethren's activities throughout the institution's existence. The Order's hospitaller role remained integral to its identity, and was enshrined in its statutes, which stated that there should always be a hospital in the Order's principal house. The hospital in Acre was governed by the Order's hospitaller and staffed by a number of physicians. This included women who joined the Order as half-sisters.[13] Pilgrims admitted to the hospital were given the opportunity to confess their sins and take the Eucharist and were provided with appropriate treatment. They ate their meals before the brethren did, representing the notion that the sick were to be treated like Christ himself. Excavations in the German quarter uncovered large numbers of ceramic sugar moulds and given the reference to the medicinal role of sugar in the Order's rule and its availability from its Galilee estates, it is likely this was used in the hospital.

Those who died within the hospital would be buried by the
brethren, who would also provide aftercare for their soul. In 1196
Pope Celestine III confirmed the Order's privilege to bury the
dead, a lucrative service to perform in the Latin East and one that
was jealously guarded by the Hospitallers. Wealthy nobles were
also prepared to pay handsomely for burial within or close to one
of Christendom's most sacred shrines. In 1216 Honorius III had
permitted the brethren to establish their own cemeteries.[14] The
Order continued to provide medical care and accommodation to
pilgrims and crusaders who visited Acre, and during the Fifth
Crusade the brethren set up a field hospital. By 1230 the Order
had at least 26 hospitals in Christendom, attesting to the importance of their role in the provision of healthcare.[15] These hospitals
were staffed by both men and women, although the statutes indicated that the latter should be housed separately and away from
the male brethren. However, the Order's military role quickly
superseded its hospitaller function and the foundation or acquisition of new hospitals was gradually curtailed. This was reflected
in the Order's rule in 1264, which stated that new hospitals
required the consent of the master and senior officials.

The Order's Final Decades in Outremer

Following Salza's death in 1239, subsequent masters continued
to manage relations between the pope and the emperor. The
brethren's leadership became split between the two factions,
which even caused a short-lived rift within the Order, but
following the resignation of the pro-imperial Poppo of Osterna
in 1256, subsequent grand masters supported the papacy. Operat-
ing in multiple theatres of war simultaneously throughout these
decades, the Order became militarily overstretched and experienced setbacks in a battle against the forces of Novgorod at Lake
Peipus in Livonia, following the insurrection in Prussia and war

with Pomerelia in 1242 (see Chapter Four). In October 1244 the Order's brethren joined what was left of the army of the Kingdom of Jerusalem, which faced the Egyptian Ayyubid force at La Forbie. Most of the brethren who fought were killed and the Ayyubid victory finally broke the military power of the crusader states. With the emerging threat of the Mamluk sultanate, the Templars, Hospitallers and Teutonic Order signed a treaty in 1258 swearing to work together to protect Outremer, and to resolve any disputes through arbitration. They would end their internal quarrels and render aid to one another at times of crisis in the northern crusader principalities of Tripoli and Antioch. Due to their relatively poor finances and limited presence in the northern Levant, the Teutonic Order's expenses were to be covered by whichever military order summoned them for aid. In 1266 the Order was even given the honorary role of inclusion in the vanguard of the crusading army of the Kingdom of Jerusalem, a position long held by the Templars and Hospitallers.

But the end was in sight. Mamluk military campaigns from 1265 steadily conquered what was left of the crusader states. Following raids on the villages around Montfort, the Order's central estate in the Galilee had declined by 1270. The Hospitallers at this time permitted the Teutonic Order to use their fields around Manueth to supply the castle at Montfort. In all likelihood the castle was under-resourced by the time the Mamluk army arrived the following year, and with the capture of Chastel Blanc, Gibelacar and the mighty fortress of Crac des Chevaliers in the preceding months, the garrison's morale was at its lowest. On 5 June 1271 the Mamluk army besieged Montfort. Archers and stone-throwers pounded away at the castle, and an attempt was made to undermine the walls. On 12 June the outer ward was taken and the garrison surrendered, although the brethren were permitted to return to Acre. On 4 July Sultan Baybars ordered the destruction of the castle to prevent it from being used

Pyramidal arrowhead from the siege of Montfort castle found during excavations in 2012.

again. Much of the complex was set on fire to weaken and bring down the structure, visible archaeologically in layers of charcoal and ash, shattered and discoloured stones and remains of charred beams. This castle was clearly of little strategic value to the Mamluks, who established their new administrative centre at Castellum Regis.

Meanwhile in Prussia, the Order finally suppressed a second major native insurrection in 1274. Following this, Grand Master Burchard of Schwanden attempted to redirect the Order's resources from the Baltic to the Holy Land, but these efforts ended with his resignation in 1290. The following year Acre fell to the Mamluks, an event that would have lasting repercussions, not just for all the military orders, but for the whole crusading movement. Most of the Order's brethren in Acre were killed during the siege, including the commander of Sicily, Henry of Bouland, who had been given the responsibility for organizing the Order's defence after Burchard of Schwanden abruptly resigned. After the siege the Order's headquarters were relocated to Venice, which had long served as one of its supply ports. But the brethren's time fighting for the Holy Land was over. Within two decades the grand master's seat was moved to Marienburg (Pol. Malbork) in Prussia, heralding a new era in the Order's history.

THREE

A New Frontier: The Teutonic Order in Transylvania

I n 1211 the Teutonic Order became involved in the defence of the eastern frontier of Hungary at the invitation of King Andrew II. Fourteen years later they would be violently expelled by the royal army. The brethren's relatively brief involvement in Transylvania has fascinated both historians and archaeologists, and remains the subject of debate, particularly as their activities have left very little evidence, represented by less than a dozen documents (largely papal correspondence) and significantly fewer archaeological sites. Some have argued the brethren's activities in Transylvania were an attempt to establish their own polity, but this view has been largely dismissed in recent scholarship.[1] This episode in the Order's history is also regarded as a prelude to its involvement in Prussia, which began in earnest in the years following the brethren's expulsion from Transylvania. There are certainly some similarities in how the Order became involved in the two regions, and the experience of the Burzenland may have informed some of the decisions made by the brethren in the early years of the Prussian Crusade, an experience that was very different from the Levant.

Hungarian princes and monarchs had long supported the military orders within their realm, and both the Hospitallers and Templars had established a dozen commanderies in the Transdanubian region by the mid-thirteenth century. In 1211 Andrew II granted estates to the Teutonic Order in the eastern part of his domain, within the region known as the Burzenland (Lat. *Terra Borsa*) in southeastern Transylvania. His intention was to establish a permanent and effective border force to guard against raids from the Cumans, a pagan Turkic nomadic group who occupied the lands north of the Black Sea. The Burzenland had been settled by the Pechenegs, who had long been tasked with protecting the eastern frontier, but had become less of an effective border force in the face of growing Cuman numbers, whose raids into Transylvania were intensifying in the early thirteenth century. Saxon migrants had also settled and established a number of towns in the region from the mid-twelfth century at the invitation of King Géza ii, but they too did not have sufficient resources to mobilize an effective defence.

The Pecheneg population was also essentially pagan, despite earlier attempts at Christianization, and Andrew intended to strengthen the Church's presence in the region with the foundation of a new Transcarpathian bishopric. Royal authority here was limited to only three castles, and by inviting the Order to secure the frontier Andrew was essentially delegating his kingdom's security in the east to the brethren. Although the Templars and Hospitallers were already established within Hungary, Andrew's choice of the Teutonic Order was probably influenced by his connections with the German aristocracy. Andrew had married Gertrude of Merania and in 1211 their daughter Elisabeth was betrothed to Ludwig, the son of the Duke of Thuringia, who in turn was a close friend of the Order's master Herman of Salza. On a more pragmatic level, the Order was the ideal choice for securing a region populated by German-speaking settlers.

Castle Building in the Burzenland

The Burzenland, at the eastern end of the kingdom of Hungary, was a highland region bounded by the Carpathian Mountains to the south and east. These mountains were only really traversable by armies through seven passes that cut through their steep slopes, and it was through here that the Cumans attacked Transylvania and Hungary. Most of the royal charters emphasized that the Order was given uninhabited land (*terra deserta*), and while there were some settlements in the region, it is evident the Order encouraged migrants to establish new colonies; the royal charter permitted the brethren to build timber castles and towns (*castra lignea et urbes ligneas*).[2] They were exempted from having to host royal officials or pay specific types of taxes, and also granted the rights to estab-lish markets, elect their own judges and keep any gold or silver found on their lands, albeit with one part handed over to the crown. In the following year, Andrew exempted the Order from further taxes owing to Cuman attacks against the newly estab-lished settlements on their lands. In 1213 William, the Bishop of Transylvania, permitted the Order to gather tithes from their subjects, providing they were not Hungarians or Székelys. The latter were an ethnically distinct Hungarian group who had played an important role in the settlement and defence of the region. Andrew also granted the brethren the newly completed castle of Kreuzburg, together with its estates. All of this provided the Order with a stable financial basis to establish themselves and a greater degree of autonomy. Yet the fact that William's decree was subsequently confirmed by Pope Honorius III has been interpreted by some scholars as the Order anticipating future conflict with the diocese, and seeking public certification of their privileges from their ecclesiastical sovereign.

The Order was clearly very successful at governing its Tran-sylvanian holdings and established a programme of resettlement for those prepared to migrate to the region, providing attractive incentives. There is documentary evidence for the construction of five castles, which were used as both military outposts and administrative centres, and at least one may have been located beyond the Carpathian Mountains. Only one of these castles has been identified in the landscape.[3] This is *Castrum Sancta Mariae* or Marienburg (today Feldioara after Hungarian *földvár*, referring to an earthwork stronghold or a prehistoric fortification, a name which appears from the fourteenth century), and was most likely the principal house of the Order in Transylvania. Named after the Order's patron, the Virgin Mary, it was built alongside an existing German settlement, where excavations of the cemetery uncovered more than a hundred graves with burial rites that were attributed to a migrant German population, who settled here in the mid-twelfth century. Marienburg then formed a nucleus for the establishment of new settlements populated by German migrants, which are documented in later sources. The castle was built on a hill on the west bank of the Olt river, separated from the adjacent settlement by a substantial moat. Although the castle ruins that are visible today are from a much later phase of building, excavations uncovered an earlier stone wall running around the edge of the hill. The eastern tower has also been attributed to the Order on the basis of its architecture, which is atypical for the region. This suggests that large parts of the structure were built from stone, with only partial elements constructed from timber. The choice of location must have been influenced by the presence of the German community, who would have provided a suitable workforce for its construction, benefiting in turn from the additional security provided by the brethren's garrison.

Various other castles have been proposed as possible candidates for the Order's strongholds, including Rucăr, Codlea, Brassovia and on Sprenghi hill by Braşov, but none has architectural details

Ruins of the castle at Feldioara, Transylvania, Romania, identified as the site of the Teutonic Order's castle of Marienburg.

that can be linked with the earlier structure in Feldioara or a distinctive masonry tradition datable to the early thirteenth century. Future archaeological investigations may shed further light on the Order's castle-building activities in the region, particularly in relation to the chronology of the associated settlement pattern. Some of these castles appear to have been founded outside the bounds of the territory granted by the Hungarian king, particularly in the Bodza region of Transcarpathia. In this respect, the Order was expanding its presence across the mountains towards the Black Sea. According to a letter from Pope Gregory ix, the Order had built a powerful stronghold in territory controlled by the Cumans, which prevented their entry into Transylvania. The Cumans attempted to capture it but were defeated, after which some allegedly accepted baptism.

Several years passed and sometime in 1221 Andrew appears to have revoked the Order's privileges. It is not clear why, but the construction of stone castles established a level of permanence

that may have been seen as a challenge to the crown. Stone
castles were rare in Hungary in the early thirteenth century
and largely associated with royal authority, while the majority
of regional fortifications were built from timber and earth. The
brethren also appeared to have expanded into lands beyond
those specified in the earlier charter, the likely end result of
conquests of territory occupied (perhaps even temporarily) by
Cumans. It is also possible that Hungarian policy towards the

Foundations of a wall most likely dating to the 13th century uncovered
during excavations at the castle in Feldioara in 2007. The wall in the
top of the image is from the rebuilding of the castle in the 14th century.

Cumans began to change at this time.[4] With Cuman attacks against Transylvania decreasing in the 1220s in the wake of the Mongol invasions, a more diplomatic approach appears to have been adopted, involving missionary activity. The first Dominican mission to the Cumans began in 1221, while the Order still controlled the Burzenland, but this did not have any tangible results. The Order, who probably still viewed the Cumans as enemies of Christendom, may have inadvertently or deliberately hindered missionary efforts and therefore compromised Andrew's attempts to bring the Cumans under his overlordship.

In any event, the king changed his mind in 1222 when he issued a new charter to the brethren, renewing the donations of 1211 and 1212. In addition, he granted them access to salt mines, exempting twelve of their vessels carrying salt from paying tolls and confirming their territorial acquisitions in southern Moldavia and northeast Wallachia. The brethren and their subjects were also exempted from taxes when travelling through the lands of the Szeklers and the Vlachs. While encouraging the Order's subjects in the Burzenland, the king forbade the resettlement of people from royal estates. Finally, the brethren were prohibited from minting coins, although they were granted the income from the annual exchange of 'new money'. It is not clear why Andrew had been so generous to the Order after almost expelling it from his lands. He noted in his charter that having previously deprived the brethren as a result of his anger, he was reimbursing them. In January 1223 the pope ordered the Bishop of Eger to appoint an archdeacon for the Burzenland, until the population had grown large enough to warrant the creation of a bishopric there. There was clearly tension with the local Church, for in December of the same year the pope rebuked the Bishop of Transylvania for exercising his jurisdiction over the Order's exempt lands in the Burzenland. As a follow-up to this, on 30 April 1224 Honorius placed the Order's lands under his protection.

Expulsion from Transylvania

In June 1225 the pope received news that the Order had been expelled from Transylvania. Andrew had entered the Burzenland with an army, causing a thousand marks' worth of damage and killing a number of the brothers and their subjects. Honorius wrote to him to ask for the Burzenland to be restored to the Order, and to inform him that a papal commission was investigating the matter. He would write twice more to the king, and in his final letter in February 1226 reiterated how the royal donation of the Burzenland had been beneficial to the Order, and by extension to the Holy Land. By this time the papal commission had confirmed the king's stated reasons for expelling the brethren: they had overreached their privileged position and occupied further royal properties without permission. The pope acknowledged this, but berated the king for expelling the Order before the conclusion of the papal investigation. In his correspondence, Honorius would single out those who were envious of the brethren's prosperity for influencing Andrew's decision and there was invariably political intrigue involved in their expulsion. The next pope, Gregory IX, continued trying to persuade Andrew to return the lands to the Order, confirmed its privileges in the Burzenland in 1231 and threatened the king and his son Béla with ecclesiastical sanctions. Ultimately, Transylvania would end up in Béla's hands. Historians continue to debate Andrew's motives, but in the absence of any direct evidence, it is only possible to speculate.

The Path to Prussia

In the summer of 1222 some brother-knights from the Teutonic Order and Templars had accompanied Henry the Bearded of Silesia on a crusade against the Prussians, after which they were granted estates in his duchy.[5] The campaign targeted the frontier

province of the *Terra Culmensis* (Ger. Kulmerland, Pol. Ziemia
chełmińska), a part of the early Polish state and subsequently the
Kuyavian-Masovian province under the lordship of Duke Konrad
of Masovia, the son of the Polish king Casimir. Konrad also participated in the crusade, along with his brother Leszek the White
of Lesser Poland and Swietopelk II of Pomerania. This Masovian
castellany had been hit hard by pagan Prussian raids in 1218
and 1220, and most of its strongholds had been destroyed. Only
the regional centre at Kulm had endured. Following the crusade
of the Polish dukes, Silesian troops garrisoned the Kulmerland's
strongholds, but were massacred by the Prussians in 1224. Raids
across the borderland into Masovia and Pomerelia continued, and
the issue confronting Konrad mirrored in some ways Andrew II's
concerns for the security of Hungary's eastern frontier.

After a short-lived civil war between the Polish dukes the
following year, Konrad invited the Teutonic Order to secure
the Masovian frontier, perhaps at the suggestion of the Duke
of Silesia. Konrad was focused on taking Cracow to enable him
to become the High Duke of Poland, and needed the Order to
provide security for his duchy. He granted them the embattled
Kulmerland, although at this time Salza was focusing on commitments in the Levant. Konrad renewed his offer and, in a charter
issued on 23 April 1228, he granted the brethren the village
of Orłów in northern Kuyavia alongside the Kulmerland. As
an added incentive, in May, Christian, the nominal Bishop of
Prussia, had granted the Order the tithe from his estates in the
Kulmerland, although this was purely a symbolic gesture as the
territory was not in the brethren's hands. That summer Konrad
and Christian lost their patience and established their own military order, the *Milites Christi de Prussia* (the Knights of Christ of
Prussia, or more commonly the Order of Dobrin, after the land
they were given), to essentially carry out the same task as envisaged for the German brethren. When the Order of Dobrin proved

to be ineffective against the Prussians, Konrad turned once more
to the Teutonic Order and issued a new charter to incentivize
the brethren in 1229.

In 1228–9 the Order had focused on the crusade of Frederick
II, during which the relationship between the emperor and the
pope had deteriorated, and Salza became involved in the peace
negotiations between the two parties. The Order, regarded as a
neutral mediator, was given the important responsibility of taking
temporary possession of both papal and imperial castles in Apulia
until a peaceful resolution had been decided. Towards the end of
the negotiations, the papal legate William of Modena arrived,
having recently been in Livonia. In all likelihood he met with
Salza and discussed the planned involvement of the Order on the
Masovian frontier. In 1230 Konrad issued two further charters to
the Order, the first of which, the so-called Treaty of Kruschwitz,
not only gave the Order the Kulmerland, but guaranteed the
brethren's independence and conferred on them the right to rule
any territories they conquered that belonged to the enemies of
the faith. For a long time, historians regarded this as a forgery,
but it was most likely prepared by a notary of the Order, with the
involvement of Salza and Modena, and signed by the duke.[6] The
second charter included a settlement at Nessau (Pol. Nieszawa)
and referred to the war against pagans. This was followed by substantial donations of property in the Kulmerland from Bishop
Christian and from the Bishop of Płock, the leading prelate of
Masovia. It is likely that Christian hoped to maintain ecclesiastical overlordship over the Order, but with the granting of further
papal privileges to the brethren he became increasingly sidelined.

The negotiations between the emperor and the pope concluded with the Peace of San Germano, and in September 1230
the pope guaranteed the Order's rights to the land granted to
them in Prussia, including any they might conquer. Papal privileges would subsequently focus on strengthening the Order

in Prussia, rather than the Levant. The Order's involvement in the wars against the Prussians, and within a few years in the lands of the other Balts, Livs and Estonians, would have a profound and lasting impact on the brethren's future.

FOUR

Holy War and Conquest: The Teutonic Order's Crusades in Prussia and Livonia

By the mid-twelfth century German, Polish and Danish magnates and prelates sought to harness the crusading movement to further their own territorial ambitions, while the papacy increasingly deployed the tool of crusade to defend missionary work and Catholic converts in the Baltic Sea region. Cistercian missionaries had followed in the footsteps of German merchants, who were keen to access the markets of the Rus' principalities. Sustained crusades against the pagan societies of the eastern Baltic began in 1198, when Innocent III issued a bull to aid the missionary work of the German Cistercian abbot Berthold among the Livs of the lower Daugava (today western Latvia).[1] A crusading army sailed from Lübeck to the region the Christians called Livonia (Ger. Livland – 'Livs' land'), but shortly afterwards Berthold was killed in a battle. His successor, Albert of Buxhövden, who took up the mantle of Bishop of Livonia (and subsequently the bishop's seat was relocated from Uexküll to Riga), led much more successful crusades and branded the conquered lands as *Terra Mariana* (the land of the Virgin Mary), with the aim of placing Livonia on a par with the Holy Land.[2] In this he was successful, for crusading in the Baltic would soon become as valued as it was in the Levant; from 1217 those participating in the war against the pagans could benefit from a full crusading indulgence.[3] After establishing the town of Riga with the aid of the local Livs and German merchants, in 1202 Albert founded his own military order, the Sword Brothers, who would lead seasonal military campaigns that by 1230 saw the subjugation of most of the territory corresponding to central-north Latvia and Estonia. Native rulers in the south held on to their autonomy through fierce resistance, as well as treaties with successive bishops. Northern Estonia had been conquered by the Danish crown, but the lands were seized by the Sword Brothers in 1227. Over time the entire region corresponding to modern Estonia and Latvia would come to be referred to as Livonia, although much of the native population survived the fighting and regional differences remained pronounced.

The Teutonic Order became actively involved in the Baltic frontier of Latin Christendom from 1230, following several years of negotiations with Konrad of Masovia. The brethren had been granted the Masovian castellany of the Kulmerland, which had been devastated and occupied by pagan Prussians.[4] Their first mission was to secure this territory by force, the start of a protracted war that would last for over fifty years. With the regular aid of crusading armies drawn from neighbouring Catholic states, particularly the Holy Roman Empire, the Order conquered all the Prussian tribal territories by 1283, despite two native insurrections and periods of warfare with Catholic Pomerelia. Later on, over the course of the fourteenth century, the brethren began to refer to the conquered lands as Prussia, including the Kulmerland and Pomerelia (annexed in 1309), and to describe themselves as the 'German Order in Prussia', a term also used by the Holy See.[5]

The Order became involved in Livonia within a few years of commencing its crusades against the Prussians. Following the death of most of the Sword Brothers at the Battle of Saule in 1236, the remainder and their holdings were incorporated into the Teutonic Order the following year. From this point the Order became involved in the internal politics of Livonia, defined by ongoing power struggles with the archbishops of Riga, the town of Riga, and to a lesser extent the bishops of Dorpat (Est. Tartu) and Ösel-Wiek. Its external politics became defined by complex and changing relations with Lithuania and the Rus' principalities of Pskov and Novgorod, as well as the vicissitudes of Danish, Swedish, papal and imperial involvement.

While the defence of Catholics and native converts was the regular justification given for the crusades in the eastern Baltic, the conquest of territory was accompanied by the imposition of ecclesiastical governance. This represented the actual implementation of the expansion of Christendom, bringing the tribal territories under the ecclesiastical overlordship of the Holy See. This developed from the onset of the crusades in Livonia, and when the Order took over the Sword Brothers' holdings it had to contend with the authority of the established episcopates. Of those, only the chapter of Courland was incorporated into the Order, strengthening the brethren's influence in southwestern Livonia. In Prussia the subdivision into dioceses, though discussed earlier, was not truly formulated until 1243. Under the papal plan, bishops would be granted a third of the territory within their dioceses in Prussia, where they were able to exercise secular as well as ecclesiastical power. Both the Order and the Dominicans sought to have their own members appointed to these positions, which began from 1245 and came to number four by the end of the thirteenth century: Kulm, Pomesania, Ermland (Warmia) and Samland (Sambia). Three of the Prussian chapters were organized under the Order's rule; the canons of Kulmsee (Pol. Chełmża) voted to adopt the rule in 1264 and the cathedral chapters of Pomesania and Samland were drawn up from the Order's own priests in 1285. This meant they swore allegiance to the grand master and were more likely to elect members of the Order as bishops. This contributed to internal political stability and facilitated the coexistence of the various theocratic dominions within

Prussia; disputes, where they occurred, were largely of a personal and financial nature. In 1255 a further challenge to the Order's control over the dioceses emerged when all the bishoprics of Prussia and Livonia came under the authority of the Archbishop of Riga.[6]

The specific events of the Baltic crusades involving the Teutonic Order are primarily known from a set of chronicles written by members of the Order: Peter of Dusburg's *Chronicle of Prussia*, later translated by Nicholas of Jeroschin for the benefit of the Order's membership, and the *Livonian Rhymed Chronicle*, as well as papal and other diplomatic correspondence. The more famous *Chronicle* by Henry of Livonia only covers events up to 1227 and was written by a cleric advocating the Bishop of Riga's position in Livonia.[7] There is also archaeological evidence, which provides both high-resolution site-specific information and broader perspectives into the cultural and environmental impact of the conquests.[8] The Baltic crusades became wars of territorial conquest, endorsed by the papacy and emperor, but they were envisaged by the Order and other Catholic commentators as both a physical and spiritual struggle, waged to defend Catholic Christendom.

The Order in Prussia

Brother-knights of the Teutonic Order began arriving on the border of Duke Konrad's territory in 1228–30, most probably from Thuringia and Saxony. In 1229 they garrisoned a small stronghold built with the assistance of the Masovians on a hill on the south bank of the Vistula, which they called Vogelsang, to use as a base for striking into the occupied Kulmerland. The following year the garrison was reinforced. Under the direction of Herman Balk, the newly appointed master of Prussia, Vogelsang's fortifications were extended downhill to the river to create a secure harbour for shipping in supplies. Konrad bestowed further privileges on the Order, including the village of Nessau (Pol. Nieszawa), which the Order fortified. Over the next few years, the Order received privileges and rights from Konrad (the 'Treaty of Kruschwitz' in 1230; 1235) the Holy See (the 'Golden Bull of Rieti' in 1234) and Emperor Frederick II (the 'Golden Bull of Rimini' probably in 1235, backdated to 1226). The latter granted the Order the same power in Prussia as wielded by an imperial prince, and may have been an attempt to limit the papal claim to suzerainty over the Order's territory outlined in the Rieti bull.[9] These cumulative donations and confirmations provided the Order with the basis for wielding secular power in the Kulmerland and the territories it would conquer over the next five decades. The brethren's authority here would be underpinned by its own military strength.

The Order's own forces on the Prussian frontier were small at this time, and alongside military aid provided by Duke Konrad, the pope supported them with crusading bulls that enabled recruitment from neighbouring regions. The Dominicans were charged with preaching the crusade and supporting the Order's efforts, and in 1231 the friars gave sermons in Magdeburg, Bremen, Poland, Pomerania, Moravia, Holstein and Gotland; in the following year this preaching was extended to Bohemia and then to other regions of Northern and Eastern Europe. In order to maximize recruitment, in February 1232 the pope authorized the granting of indulgences to those who attended the Dominicans' crusading sermons.[10] In the spring of 1231 the Order's brethren crossed the Vistula with Masovian forces into

overleaf: Unknown artist, *Arrival of the Teutonic Knights in the Kulmerland*, 1713, oil on wood. The painting illustrates the story of the foundation of the first stronghold built by the Order in the Kulmerland from the chronicle of Peter of Dusburg. According to the story, the knights fortified an oak tree at Thorn and are shown here defending it against the Prussians, who are represented as Saracens.

Dort in dem Culmer Land stund ein sehr grosse Eichen,
An Weixel Flusses Strand, so nicht hett ihres gleichen.
Darauf baut ein Castell, Hermannus Balcke klueg:
Gleich aus ein Citadell, scharpf in die Feinde schluug:
Die Eiche war das Thor, wardurch der Teische Orden,
Sestigen so Empor, und Herr Des Preüssen worden.

Der Erste Kampf diß war, so kostet Würth, vnd Spott,
Ja Leib, vnd Leben gar: Vil Edler Ritter Blutt:
Ob schon ein harten Thorn, der Orden da erlitten;
Doch d'Ritter außerkorn, wie Risen dapfer stritten:
Würth nach erlegt'n Feünd: daselbst Sie dan ein Statt
Erbauten: die noch heünd, den Nahmen Thorn hatt.

the Kulmerland, attacking Prussian bases and refortifying the castellany's abandoned strongholds. The Order's military successes in Prussia have been attributed to superior equipment, particularly the use of heavy war horses and crossbows, effective discipline and ultimately their reputation on the battlefield.[11] In fact, crusader and Prussian armies were similarly equipped, but thanks to the mechanism of crusading, the Order benefited from a regular stream of military support with each campaign. After fulfilling their obligations, most crusaders returned home, leaving the Order's brethren to maintain garrisons with their subjects. The defeated Prussians were given the choice to convert to Catholicism, accept the authority of the Order and the Catholic Church, provide military service and pay taxes and tithes. The Order's early activities provide a glimpse of how the brethren rapidly became involved not only in securing the region militarily, with the construction of timber and earth strongholds, but in managing the establishment, layout and development of settlements, as well as facilitating the provisioning of their inhabitants and animals. These were derived from resident Masovian and converted Prussian communities, supplemented by Polish and German migrants. The Order's approach to organizing its newly acquired territories was incremental and reactive, with settlements being relocated and castles dismantled once they were no longer strategically useful. These castle towns solidified the Order's presence in the conquered territories, as they would in Livonia, providing economic and military support for their governance.

Conquering the Kulmerland

In 1231 the Order founded its first settlement at Thorn (from Latin Thorun, derived from an early Slavic term for 'worn path'; Pol. Toruń), most probably in relation to a crossing point across the Vistula, just west of Nessau, where a fortified bridgehead to the Kulmerland was established. Within a few years flooding resulted in its relocation to higher ground further east, to where the Old Town of Toruń is located today. Here the Order built a castle within the ruins of a Masovian stronghold on an out-crop overlooking a crossing over the river, transferring the name Thorn to the new site.[12] In 1232 the Order built the stronghold of Potterberg, which has been identified with the final phase of the site of Kałdus, where a Teutonic Order bracteate was uncovered in excavations: the centre of the Masovian castellany of Kulm.[13] This would later be dismantled and the materials used to build the castle at Mewe (Pol. Gniew). In the same year, the brethren fortified Althaus, where recent excavations uncovered traces of the earliest timber and earth stronghold, before its

The principal routes of the Prussian Crusade, 1230–83.

replacement by the later castle.[14] The Order issued its first charter
to the settlement of Kulm in 1233, which formed the template
for the 'Kulm Law', which the brethren would use to define the
privileges and obligations of the majority of chartered settlements in Prussia. In 1239 Kulm was relocated to what is today
the district of Rybaki in Chełmno; by the 1240s the Order had
constructed a castle by the town. Flooding prompted yet another
relocation to higher ground, where the layout of the town took
on a regular plan following the new 'Kulm foot'.

Crusading in western Prussia

Within a few years, the Order had secured the bounds of the
Kulmerland, and its armies began to advance northwards, following the Vistula into Pomesania. This region was a borderland
between the Pomeranians and the Prussians, and the Order
built a stronghold on a fenland isle they named Marienwerder
(Pol. Kwidzyn) in 1233. This structure was later relocated to
the top of the nearby escarpment and a settlement established
alongside it. This became the base for further attacks into
Pomesania and Pogesania. In the meantime, the Prussians ab-
ducted Bishop Christian and imprisoned him for five years,
removing the most vocal opponent of the Order's territorial
governance of the conquered territories. The bishop's settlement and missionary base at Zantir (or Santyr), on the right bank
of the Vistula's tributary, the Nogat, was acquired by the Order
at this time and would become a major administrative centre for
Pomesania. This has been identified with the multi-period

Teutonic Order bracteates recovered from Biała Góra.

Ruins of the castle at Radzyń Chełmiński, Poland (Rehden, Prussia).

settlement discovered near the village of Biała Góra.[15] Briefly taken by the Pomerelian duke during his war with the Order in the early 1240s, it was returned to the brethren in 1248–9, and the convent here would eventually be relocated to Marienburg (Pol. Malbork) three decades later. In 1234 the construction of strongholds at Rehden (Radzyń Chełmiński) and Graudenz (Pol. Grudziądz) secured the Kulmerland further, while the winter campaign of that year saw the capture of the Pomesanian stronghold at 'Castle Hill' (Góra Zamkowa) near Alt Christburg, which the Order refortified.[16] This, in turn, became a mustering point for further campaigns. The stronghold would lose its significance in 1248 with the establishment of (new) Christburg (Pol. Dzierzgoń), a few kilometres away, as the headquarters of the

Order's commandery as well as the residence of the Order's hospitaller.

In 1237 the crusading army, led by Count Henry of Meissen, sailed down the Nogat to the Elbing river, where in the winter the Order constructed a timber stronghold in the place later referred to as Herrenpfeil, an island in the river. The following year, the nearby settlement now referred to as Elbing (Pol. Elbląg), populated with migrants, many of whom came from Lübeck, was furnished with a Dominican friary. Reluctantly the Order permitted the town to acquire the Lübeck Law sometime in 1240, which would give its merchant families greater autonomy. In 1239–40 work started on rebuilding the timber castle in brick and stone, along with a church. This would become the residence of the provincial master and the Order's political centre in Prussia from 1251 through to 1309. It would also become the main base for leading crusades into Warmia. The Order consolidated its military successes here with the construction of a stronghold in Balga.

Prussian insurrection and war with Pomerelia

In 1238 a war between Duke Swietopelk of Pomerelia and his brother Sambor disrupted the Order's supply lines on the Vistula. Swietopelk, considering both the Order (who supported Sambor) and Poland as threats, allied with the Prussians and this instigated a regionwide attack on the brethren's strongholds and towns in Warmia, Natangia and Bartia in 1242. Prussian attacks were even able to reach the Kulmerland, and during this time the Order lost control of most of its strongholds and the territories it had conquered, with the exception of Balga, Elbing, Rehden, Kulm and Thorn. The brethren were able to gain support from the Polish dukes, as well as military aid from the margraves of Meissen and Brandenburg. The war ended with the Treaty of Christburg on 7 February 1249, mediated by the papal chaplain Jacob Pantaléon, Archdeacon of Liège (later Urban iv). The Order agreed to give all Prussian converts their personal freedom in exchange for their obedience, as well as the opportunity to join their ranks as brethren. In exchange, the Prussians had to abandon polygamy, build churches and end pagan practices, particularly those associated with funerals. The peace did not hold, and Swietopelk continued to fight against the Order until a further truce was agreed in 1253. In the meantime, the Order's system of territorial governance developed. In 1246 Grand Master Henry of Hohenlohe initiated reforms of the administrative structure of the Order in Prussia, introducing the system of commanderies.

The conquest of eastern Prussia

The Order steadily took control over the organization of the Baltic crusades. Pope Alexander iv had allowed the Order to choose their own preachers from among the Dominicans, and subsequently preaching required the Order's direct consent. Then, the Order's own priests were permitted to release crusaders from vows and grant them indulgences. In 1243, following the election of Pope Innocent iv, the Order requested further crusading bulls for Livonia and Prussia. For the first time, the pope granted the Order the ability to recruit crusaders for its ongoing war in Prussia at its own discretion, without the requirement of public preaching and with no expiration on this permission. In this respect the Order was permitted to organize a perpetual crusade in Prussia, although it continued to ask for papal permission for new crusades. By the 1260s the Order's priests were permitted to preach crusades.[17] In this way the Order gained complete control over the timing and recruitment of its campaigns.

After a final peace had been made with Pomerelia, the Order turned to the conquest of the tribal territory of Natangia, which would take some two years. In 1254 the Order's Livonian brethren launched an unsuccessful assault from Memel into Samland. That winter the largest crusading army to enter Prussian lands, which included forces from Bohemia and Brandenburg, joined the Order in a crusade against the Sambians. Within a few days the surviving Sambians had accepted baptism, sworn allegiance to the Order and offered up hostages. The Bohemian king Ottokar II sponsored the building of a fortification overlooking the Pregel river, which was named Königsberg (Rus. Kaliningrad). Within a year this had developed into a fortified convent with an associated settlement.

The Sambian nobility who had sworn loyalty to the Order had their lands and privileges confirmed, serving under the same conditions as immigrant German knights. This enabled the Order to begin military incursions into pagan Samogitia from both its northern and southern borders. Samogitia was ethnically and politically aligned with Lithuania. In 1257–9 a truce was arranged enabling Livonian and Prussian merchants to travel throughout Samogitia, and pagan Samogitians to travel freely in the domains of the Order. But when the truce expired, the Samogitians, inspired by the resistance of the Sudovians against the crusades of the Prince of Galicia and Duke of Masovia, attacked Courland in southern Livonia, prompting uprisings among the native Semigallians and Curonians, as well as attacks from the Lithuanians.

The great Prussian uprising

In September 1260 a second regionwide insurrection by the Prussians presented the most serious challenge to the Order's control of the conquered lands. The uprising was led by Henry (or Herkus) Monte, a Natangian noble. During the crusading campaign of 1240, Monte had been captured and taken back to Magdeburg for re-education, and in the early 1250s he had

gained extensive military experience fighting alongside the Order
against the eastern Prussian tribes. This experience enabled him
to mount an effective challenge to the Order. The uprising began
in the eastern Prussian territories of Samland, Natangia, Bartia
and Warmia, where the Prussians killed German priests, merchants and settlers, as well as those natives who were loyal to the
Order. Subsequently, Prussian guerrilla warfare inflicted heavy
losses on the Order's garrisons and crusading armies. As the uprising spread into western Prussia the pope called for a new crusade.
A crusading army arrived from the Rhineland and made its way
to Königsberg, defeating the besieging Sambian army. But when
the crusaders departed, the Sambians renewed their siege of the
castle. Königsberg held out, some garrisons from other castles such
as Barthenstein (Pol. Bartoszyce) were able to escape, while most
of the garrison of Kreuzburg (Rus. Slavskoye) was killed. Castles
continued to resist attacks but most fell, with Barthenstein holding out into 1264. In 1262 the Sudovians invaded Masovia and
the Lithuanians joined in attacking eastern Poland and western
Prussia, with the attacks reaching the Kulmerland and Kuyavia.
During a battle against the Natangians, the master of Prussia, the
marshal and many seasoned brother-knights were killed. The
attacks on Kulm intensified, and a large Lithuanian army entered
Masovia, Pogesania and eventually Kulm.

Despite losses such as Marienwerder, the Order's surviv-
ing garrisons held out against the Prussians. The convent at
Königsberg kept the Sambians in check and enabled more for-
tifications to be constructed. In 1265–6 substantial crusading
armies arrived from the empire. In the meantime, the sons of
Duke Swietopelk, Mestwin and his brother, declared war on the
Order. In 1267 King Ottokar of Bohemia returned to Prussia
with a large crusading army, having been promised the lands of
Sudovia and Galindia, which as yet did not belong to the Order.
The king forced Mestwin to make peace with the Order, but by

then the ice was thawing and it became virtually impossible to launch military expeditions through Prussia.

In the 1270s the Order launched raids from its castles along the Vistula and Pregel rivers, and across the northern coast. Pogesania remained the most contested region, and in 1271 the Bartians embarked on a military incursion to break the Order's hold on the region but were repelled by the garrisons at Christburg and Elbing. Shortly after, a large force of Sudovians and Lithuanians entered Kulm but failed to penetrate the town's defences, and the Bartian leader was killed after trying to storm the Order's outpost near Schönsee (Pol. Kowalewo Pomorskie), which prompted his army to disperse. The following winter, refreshed by German reinforcements, the crusading armies converged on Natangia, assaulted Henry Monte's principal stronghold and devastated the region. Monte and the leader of the Warmians were captured soon after and executed. Fighting was now concentrated on the wetlands and forests of Pogesania, where the remnants of the Prussian uprising had regrouped. In 1274 the Order finally cornered its enemies at Heilsberg (Pol. Lidzbark Warmiński). A further insurrection in 1277 prompted the Order to enter Pogesania and resettle part of its population, while some fled to Samogitia. The brethren spent the following years conquering Nadruvia and Sudovia. By 1283 the latter region was reduced to a wilderness, as the population either fled to Lithuania or was resettled to the west by the Order. Easternmost Sudovia remained a frontier between the Order and Lithuania, frustrating Polish efforts at political expansion, which had been underpinned by a series of attacks on the region from 1264 to 1282.[18]

The Order in Livonia

On 22 September 1236 an army led by the Sword Brothers confronted a combined force of Samogitians and Semigallians at the Battle of Saule, in north Lithuania. The Livonian army, unable to manoeuvre its heavy cavalry effectively in the marshes, was soundly defeated and the majority of the Sword Brothers were killed, including their master Volkwin. The following year, with papal approval and following the agreement of the general chapter that met in Marburg in June, the Teutonic Order integrated the remnants of the Sword Brothers into their ranks and took over their holdings, which included a number of castles. The Order sent some six hundred personnel, including around sixty brother-knights, to Livonia. In the process the brethren inherited the Sword Brothers' dispute with the bishops of Riga regarding their subordination to the episcopal see. This originated from at least 1207, when the Sword Brothers had received a third of the conquered territories, which was confirmed by Pope Innocent III three years later, stipulating the bishop's ecclesiastical and secular overlordship over the military order. After acquiring land within the episcopates of Dorpat and Ösel-Wiek, the Sword Brothers also became subjugated to their bishops.

When the Sword Brothers approached the Teutonic Order in the 1230s to discuss a possible merger, they were hoping it would have a positive effect on their governance of their lands – perhaps a means of retaining the territories they had seized in Estonia and southern Livonia, but more importantly providing them with much-needed financial support.[19] Albert's death in 1229 prompted a crisis over the governance of Livonia, which led to the Sword Brothers' occupation of north Estonia, while the Curonians sought treaties directly with the pope, who aimed to preserve the freedom of converts. The intervention of the papal legate Baldwin of Alna, who took Estonia and Courland under the Holy See's protection, ultimately led to a military confrontation in 1234 with the Sword Brothers, who had gathered a coalition of Livonian forces. Subsequently, William of Modena re-divided the conquered lands between the Teutonic Order and the three Livonian bishoprics (Riga, Dorpat, Ösel-Wiek), while the smaller bishopric of Courland was also formally established.

A year after incorporating the Sword Brothers into its ranks, the Order agreed to hand back north Estonia to the Danish crown and to split the territory gained from future conquests. In exchange, King Valdemar would provide the Order with military support and grant them the district of Jerwia, the only territory that was independent from any Livonian bishop. The agreement to collaborate on future crusades soon bore fruit. William of Modena had been urging a crusade against Novgorod in his desire to unify the western and eastern churches. In 1240 the crusading host, including vassals of the Danish king and a large contingent of the Order's brother-knights, took control of Pskov and from there attacked the territories of Novgorod in the winter, reaching the town's suburbs. They only held this temporarily before Prince Alexander Nevsky took the city and then defeated the crusading army at the 'Battle on the Ice' on the frozen Lake Peipus on 5 April 1242. This halted the Order's eastward advance, fixing the border between the Catholic and Eastern Orthodox worlds, although minor clashes with Novgorod and Pskov would continue. Following this, the Livonian brethren turned their attention to the south, where they were obliged to fight a defensive war for several decades.

During this time their focus would remain largely on the consolidation of their existing territory. This saw investment in castle construction, building on the commanderies established by the Sword Brothers and creating new centres in the south in response to the threats from Lithuania. The most

Ruins of the conventual castle at Viljandi (Fellin), Estonia.

important house was located in Riga, but in 1250 a new castle
was constructed in Fellin (Est. Viljandi), which would become
one of the strongest in Livonia.[20] Significant investment in this
phase of the castle is evident from the numerous early Gothic
column capitals found within the ruins,[21] reused in the later convent building constructed at the end of the thirteenth century.
Fellin would become the second largest convent in Livonia after
Riga. In the last decades of the thirteenth century smaller castles
were constructed such as Karkus (Est. Karksi) in southern Estonia,
where the earliest archaeological deposits date from about 1260
to 1293, with intensive building activities commencing in the
1280s.[22]

Courland and Semigallia

Not long after inheriting the Sword Brothers' political and territorial legacy, the Order would soon come into conflict with
the other parties involved in Livonia, which filed complaints
about it to the Holy See. In 1240 Gregory IX had castigated the

brethren for impeding the spread of Catholicism by preventing converts from attending religious services and building churches; instead, they had tasked their native subjects with manual labour. Similar charges had been previously levelled against the Sword Brothers, whose actions in Courland had prompted the native population to break from its earlier alliance. In 1242–4 the Order's forces reoccupied Courland and established the convent of Goldingen (Latv. Kuldīga). At this time the Order amalgamated the chapter of the Courland bishopric, strengthening its hold on the region. Following renewed conflict, the brethren occupied Courland again in 1253 and subdivided the territory between themselves and the episcopate. Goldingen was consolidated after peace was established in 1267.

In the 1240s the Semigallians had made a pact with the Order, which included converting to Catholicism, to aid them against Samogitian attacks. In 1251 Mindaugas, the Grand Duke of Lithuania, converted to Catholicism and allied himself with the Order in Livonia, intending to crown himself king. In exchange for facilitating his baptism and supporting his coronation, the Order demanded territory and Mindaugas gave them land in Samogitia. The following year the Order constructed a castle at Memel (Lith. Klaipėda), creating a foothold from which they could also support their brethren's attack on Samland. Within a couple of years, a town had developed alongside the castle. This was intended to serve as the base to unify the Order's territories in Prussia and Livonia. In 1256 the Samogitians attacked Memel, and the following year asked for a two-year truce, with the promise of accepting German merchants and missionaries, an agreement supported by the merchants of Riga. The peace did not outlast the truce, and in 1259 the Samogitians were raiding Courland again.

When the Order was defeated by a Samogitian force at the Battle of Schoden (Lith. Skuodas), with the death of 33 brother-knights, an emergency military tax (seven times the normal amount) was imposed on the Semigallians, which they refused to pay. The Order responded by strengthening its forces, building castles at Doblen (Latv. Dobele) and Karshowen as bases for controlling the region, and besieging the native stronghold of Terweten (Latv. Tērvete). The Samogitians came to the aid of the Semigallians, but failed to take the Order's strongholds. The following year the Curonians joined the Samogitians in their conflict against the brethren. In July 1260 the Order's combined Prussian-Livonian force suffered a catastrophic defeat at the Battle of Durbe. The Livonian master Burchard of Hornhausen was killed, along with the Prussian marshal. The outcome prompted new insurrections from the Öselians, Curonians, Semigallians and Prussians, and even Mindaugas turned against the Order, expelling and killing Christians in his realm and destroying the cathedral he had commissioned. Conflict continued in southern Livonia, while in 1267 the Order allied with the Bishop of Dorpat to fend off a Rus' attack on eastern Estonia.

In the winter of 1269–70 a Lithuanian army entered Livonia and crossed over the frozen sea to the island of Ösel (Est. Saaremaa). The Order's master Otto of Lutterberg led an army, which included troops from Danish Estonia, to meet them on 16 February on the ice between the mainland and the island of Muhu. In the ensuing Battle of Karuse, the master and a large number of brother-knights were killed. The new master, Walter of Nordeck, was able to secure help from the Order's Prussian brethren and captured a number of strongholds that had enabled the Lithuanian army to reach the coast. In 1271 this included Terwerten, which passed under the Order's control, forcing the Semigallians to agree to a truce. Then, in 1273 the Livonian master ordered the construction of a castle at Dünaburg (Latv. Daugavpils), situated on the Daugava in the far southeastern corner of Livonia. This would serve as a base for future attacks into Lithuania, shift the focus of Lithuanian forces from the western side of Livonia, and consolidate the territory the Order had acquired in the region of Lettigallia.

In 1279 the Semigallians allied with the Lithuanians and took back Terwerten. Two years later the Order would surround the stronghold with a substantial army, prompting the Semigallians to agree to another truce and to pay taxes. This peace did not last long. Eventually, in the winter of 1285–6, the Order constructed the castle of Heiligenberg (Latv. Svetkalns) across from Terwerten. Both the Samogitians and Semigallians attempted to destroy this castle, but with no success. Eventually Terwerten would be abandoned, and in 1290 hostilities in Semigallia officially ceased with the surrender of the last territory of Sidrabene. The southern part of the region became depopulated as the survivors fled into Samogitia, and the Order would only establish new centres here in the early decades of the fourteenth century. The settlement pattern in southern Semigallia collapsed by the end of the thirteenth century and the region was not repopulated until the second half of the fifteenth century and the sixteenth.[23] Similarly in south Courland an absence of native place names from the thirteenth century points to depopulation in what became the frontier with Samogitia.[24]

Now the brethren could focus on the development of their territorial governance. In August 1290, at the meeting of the general chapter of the Order's Livonian branch, the organization of the Curonian commanderies of Windau (Latv. Ventspils) and Goldingen was defined. Supplies for these convents, which were also dependent on each other, were to be drawn from a range of territories in Livonia, including the island of Ösel. The document explicitly stated that the convents had to be self-sufficient and separated from each other, each with its own food and lands, while acknowledging their role within the Order's hierarchical structure.

The Order's attention would next shift to Riga. In 1251 Albert Suerbeer, an antagonist of the Order and proponent of papal authority in the Baltic, was finally appointed to the metropolitan see of Riga and became its first archbishop. He now had episcopal jurisdiction over the dioceses of both Prussia and Livonia. In the following two decades the Order would clash with Albert over various issues, including his policy towards the Rus' principalities and his appointment of the troublesome Gunzelin of Schwerin as his personal advocate. When Gunzelin left Livonia to raise troops to fight against the Order, the master arrested the archbishop and imprisoned him. Gunzelin was told not to return, and Albert eventually recognized the Order's authority. In 1274 the Order gained imperial ratification of its rule over Riga, which resulted in open conflict that was not fully resolved until 1330 when the town surrendered to the brethren. Throughout much of the fourteenth century the Archbishop of Riga and at least one bishop of Dorpat demanded the Order swear allegiance to them as their vassals.

FIVE

Territorial Lords: The Teutonic Order's Rule in the Baltic

The conquest of pagan tribal lands in the eastern Baltic over the course of the thirteenth century resulted in the creation of new Catholic polities: Livonia and Prussia. From the 1230s the crusades had been led by the Teutonic Order, which gradually established itself as a sovereign power in Prussia, while contesting its subordinated status to the Livonian episcopates it inherited from the Sword Brothers. In both regions, the governance of the conquered territories was shared with bishops and their cathedral chapters, with north Estonia controlled by the Danish crown. Following the loss of Acre in 1291, the Order shifted its focus to its Baltic provinces, acquiring new territories in the first half of the fourteenth century; in 1309 it annexed Danzig (Pol. Gdańsk) and Pomerelia and in 1346 it purchased the Duchy of Estonia from the Danish king Valdemar IV, after suppressing the 'St George's Night' native uprising.

An International Religious Corporation

Prussia would become the most important province for the Order politically, even though only a quarter of its houses in total were located there. This prominence was largely due to the relocation of the grand master's residence to western Prussia from Venice in 1309, which became permanently established at Marienburg (Pol. Malbork) from 1324 until it was relocated to Königsberg

(Rus. Kaliningrad) in 1456. The Prussian branch also dominated the brethren's ongoing war with Samogitia and Lithuania, and later with Poland-Lithuania. Nonetheless, the Order's principal resources were derived from its substantial holdings in the empire, which increased in importance with the shift of the brethren's activities from the Levant to the Baltic. Here, the Order governed estates, but also built hospitals and churches, playing an important role in the provision of medical and pastoral care. Its properties yielded valuable rents for the organization as a whole, but its bailiwicks would also provide the recruits for the brethren's convents in Prussia and Livonia. In the process the Order strengthened its ties with imperial noble families and became heavily involved in the politics of the empire.[1] The Order also maintained a general procurator in the papal court, who was accountable to the grand master and regularly lobbied the Holy See for support against the brethren's enemies.

The Order's lands in Prussia and Livonia have been variously referred to as a monastic, theocratic or crusader state, as well as the 'Order's state' (Ger. *Ordensstaat*, Pol. *Państwo Zakonne*). Given that the Order's domains did not quite function in the same way as a contemporary secular state, the term *Ordensland* (Order's land) has also been used in the scholarly literature.[2] While the name *Terra Mariana* (the land of the Virgin Mary) predated the Order's arrival in Livonia,[3] the Virgin was considered as the sovereign of both regions and featured widely in the Order's religious and political symbolism.[4] The brethren devoted considerable resources to the conflict with Samogitia and Lithuania throughout the fourteenth century as part of their crusading ethos (see Chapter Seven), but they also increased their territorial acquisitions with the annexation of Pomerelia in 1308–10, temporarily acquired a number of small territories in Masovia, including the Dobrin Land, Wizna Land and Zawkrze Land, and purchased the Neumark in 1402, which remained in the Order's possession until 1455.[5] The Order also became involved in the geopolitics of the Baltic Sea region. This included the grand master's membership of the Hanse, actions against piracy and the short-lived governance of the island of Gotland. During this time, the figure of the grand master became increasingly prominent and by the late fourteenth century his residence in Marienburg had become the equivalent of a major European court.[6] The importance of the Livonian and German masters also steadily increased, and in the Order's imperial heartlands the latter almost came to rival the grand master.[7] Nonetheless, the Order remained a religious corporation where power was organized collectively and reinforced through the monastic precepts of obedience, celibacy and the renunciation of personal property.

The Order's military resources were clearly instrumental in securing the conquest of lands in the eastern Baltic, and this provided the basis upon which a widely held perception of its legitimate governance was based. This was underpinned by the introduction of new laws and the creation of new relationships with its subjects, both conquered native peoples and incoming migrants, through the granting of land and privileges. The Order became the dispenser of justice and exercised the right to levy taxes from its subjects, which included control over minting rights. The coinage issued by the Order became standardized and emphasized the authority of the grand master in Prussia, and of the provincial master in Livonia, but the most visible expressions of the brethren's overlordship were their castles, particularly the largest, which were fortified convents (see Chapter Six).

The Order's Evolving Structure

In the Baltic the Order's system of territorial governance, derived from land management practices in the Levant and Europe, evolved in response to the challenge of its growing holdings

obtained through incremental conquest and treaties.[8] In the early
decades of its involvement in Prussia, the conquered territories
were governed by a preceptor and his deputy, the equivalent of a
provincial master, with a marshal and provisors.[9] The first commanderies were delineated in Livonia with Wenden (Latv. Cēsis)
in 1237 following its acquisition from the Sword Brothers, then
Leal (Est. Lihula) in 1242, Fellin (Est. Viljandi) in 1248, and
Goldingen (Latv. Kuldīga) and Ascheraden (Latv. Aizkraukle) in
1252. Riga's commander is first mentioned in 1253, although the
convent had already long existed. The first Prussian commandery
is mentioned at Elbing (Pol. Elbląg) in 1246, but the standardi-
zation of a system of territorial organization has been attributed
to the Order's German master, Eberhard of Sayn. During his visit
to Prussia in 1251–2 he renewed the charters of Kulm and Thorn
and contributed to the designation of the convent at Elbing as
the provincial headquarters of Prussia, as well as the foundation
of the commanderies of Balga and Christburg (Pol. Dzierzgoń).[10]
This heralded the start of a more clearly defined and hierarchical
system of territorial organization.[11] By this time the Kulmerland
was clearly defined as a singular territory, subdivided into commanderies, which was governed by a provincial master first
named in 1248, a post that was abolished in the third decade of
the fourteenth century.[12]

The Order's convents

At the centre of each commandery was a convent, which housed
a nominally regular number of brothers as established in the
Order's Rule – twelve, representing the apostles – although this
figure could vary dramatically between convents and over time.[13]
Throughout the existence of the Order's Baltic branches these
brethren were all immigrants, recruited from the lower nobility
in the Order's bailiwicks in the Rhineland, middle Germany
(especially Westphalia) and southwest Germany.[14] The convent

was headed by the commander, appointed to the office for at least one year but usually more. Commanders were regularly rotated between houses, with the result that individuals gained experience of the Order's administration and contributed to its cohesion. He was supported by a *Hauskomtur* or 'house commander', who often ran the daily business of the convent. The brother-knights were served by one or more priests and non-ordained clerics, and grand masters, provincial masters and commanders had personal chaplains who accompanied them on their travels. This group was responsible for organizing the convent's religious life, but some also held diocesan roles. The conventual community also included brother-sergeants, who wore a black cross on a grey habit, as well as soldiers, servants and administrators.[15] Since the Order's convents became centres of economic activities, this necessitated the appointment of conventual officials from among the brethren to oversee specific functions. The most important included those in charge of food storage, the kitchen, granaries, the wagon store, stables, the smithy and clothing, but larger convents prompted the development of more diverse roles tailored to their specific needs.

The shape and size of commanderies varied as a result of their specific historical development, initially reflecting the subdivision of territory following military conquest or acquisition, then by reorganization, rationalization and expansion. In the densely settled Kulmerland there were also irregular districts, such as individual villages, farms or other small territories that had their own, distinct administrative status.[16] A good example of these administrative reconfigurations is represented by the short-lived commandery of Welsas, at the centre of which was the castle of Starkenberg, situated on the Osa river in the northern Kulmerland. Built in the early fourteenth century and named after an earlier stronghold on the opposite bank of the river (in turn named after the Order's main castle in the Holy Land) that

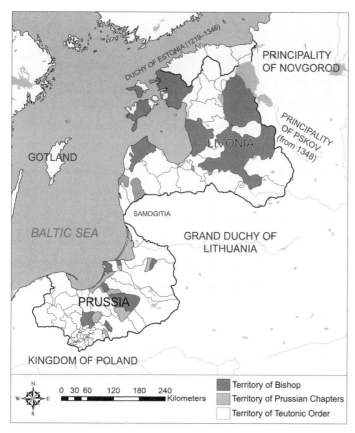

The Order's territories in the medieval Baltic, with boundaries in
Prussia from c. 1400 and Livonia c. 1450, including the outline of
the former Danish Duchy of Estonia, which was sold to the Teutonic
Order in 1346.

had been destroyed during the Prussian insurrection in 1272,
when this territorial unit was dissolved in the 1340s Starkenberg
was downgraded and reduced to a small, fortified mill. Territorial
administration would instead be handed to the advocate (Ger.
Vogt) at Rogasen (Pol. Rogoźno).[17] By about 1300 the Order had
subdivided its Livonian lands into 22 commanderies and advocateships (Ger. *Vogtei*), and its Prussian lands into 31.[18] New
major districts would be largely created with further territorial

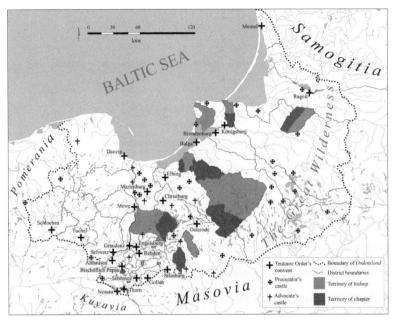

The commanderies and episcopal domains in Prussia in the
14th century.

expansion, particularly the annexation of Pomerelia in 1308–10
and the acquisition of north Estonia in 1346.

As the governance of territory became increasingly complex,
smaller districts came to be governed by advocates, procurators (Ger. *Pflegerämter*) and bailiffs (Ger. *Kammerämter*). These
officials served the role of judges, tax collectors and military
organizers, and managed provisioning and trade networks, and
the exploitation of natural resources. Advocates are first
mentioned in Livonia, where they became subordinated to
individual commanders or the master, while they are documented in eastern Prussia from the 1270s. They were initially
appointed to manage judicial and economic matters so that
commanders could focus on organizing military resources, but
some became important governors in their own right. The first
procurators are associated with the Prussian castles of Lochstedt

(Rus. Pavlovo) and Gollub (Pol. Golub) before 1309,[19] but from
the 1320s more semi-autonomous advocateships and procu-
ratorships were created in Prussia, which were directly under
the control of the grand masters and designed to bolster their
income, as dues collected in their districts would be sent directly
to Marienburg. Within a few decades, commanders in eastern
Prussia and Pomerelia were also delegating the management of
defined territories within their districts to procurators. Below
these officials in the Order's hierarchy were bailiffs (Ger. sing.
Kammer), who governed districts that included between 15 and
45 villages.[20] For the management of densely wooded districts
(Ger. *Waldämter*) in Prussia, the specialized office of forest master
(Ger. sing. *Waldmeister*) was created. All of these lesser offices
were used on an ad hoc basis in Prussia by grand masters and
commanders, depending on their needs. Above all, this administrative system was a flexible means of organizing settlement
and the economic resources required to sustain this.

Grand masters and masters

The grand master was not a monarchical ruler, but presided over
a hierarchical religious corporation where major policy decisions
were made by assemblies of the Order's members called chapters. The most important chapter included the Order's highest
officers who elected the grand master. These were the grand
commander, grand marshal, grand hospitaller, grand quartermaster and treasurer, who had previously been part of the same
convent in Acre and Venice, but from the 1320s were dispersed
to other major convents in western Prussia and after 1457 in
eastern Prussia. The provincial chapters, which included all the
Order's regional leaders, met annually and were the most effective in directing domestic and foreign policy, while the general
chapter, which theoretically included all the Order's members,
met less frequently and attendance was always incomplete.

When the grand master's seat was relocated to Marienburg in 1309, the office of Prussian master was dissolved and its last holder, Henry of Plötzke, was reappointed as marshal. This left two provincial masters in charge of the Order's Livonian and imperial territories. The Livonian master was based in Riga and from the late fifteenth century in Wenden, supported by his deputy, the marshal based in Segewold (Latv. Sigulda). The German master was based in various houses and governed the twelve bailiwicks spread across imperial lands north of the Alps. Beneath him were land commanders (Ger. *Landkomture*), who took charge of discrete territories, and below them were the district commanders. This organizational structure proved to function very effectively and would be imitated by the German Hospitallers. From about 1366, with the exception of Bozen (Ital. Bolzano) in the southern Tyrol, which was subservient to the grand master, the German master also took over responsibility for the Order's scattered Mediterranean bailiwicks, although by the end of the fifteenth century the Order had lost its Apulian and Sicilian houses.[21] At this time, dovetailing with the Order's policy of selecting its leadership from imperial magnates, the German master was elevated to the status of an imperial prince in 1494. This led to attempts to territorialize the Order's German lands, with the result that Mergentheim in Franconia essentially became a self-contained entity.[22]

Over the course of the fourteenth century the grand masters, particularly Winrich of Kniprode, sought to centralize the Order's administration. As a result, they became important political figureheads, while still being elected officials of a religious corporation. Technically they were elected for life, although a number resigned, some were dismissed by their chapter, one was assassinated (Werner of Orseln in 1330) and one famously died in battle (Ulrich of Jungingen in 1410). With the relocation of the headquarters to Marienburg, a chancellery was established which began to issue and archive documents relating to the Order's administration. Correspondence was bilingual, with Latin used into the fifteenth century, while German became more frequently used from the mid-fourteenth century. Convents would maintain updated inventories, copies of which were sent to Marienburg and collated from 1400 as 'The Great Book of Offices' (*Das Grosse Ämterbuch*), which provided a detailed overview of the Order's resources.[23] But active control over the Order's Baltic houses and European bailiwicks was maintained through a system of visitations and inspections.

When the Order purchased the Duchy of Estonia, the grand master ultimately exercised overlordship over the duchy, but over the course of the fifteenth century individual commanders, as well as the provincial master, exercised more autonomy in Livonia, which became accentuated with the privatization of conventual property. This trend was also visible in the region's episcopates, with bishops treating their offices as private domains.[24] The production of separate Prussian and Livonian literature within the Order emphasizing regional histories also points to a degree of separation within the Order's structure. In a further expression of the friction between the Order's branches, given that the procurator in the papal court was essentially the grand master's representative, the Livonian and German masters would ultimately send their own envoys to the Holy See, the former already in the fourteenth century, the latter in the fifteenth.[25]

Governing Natives and Migrants

With the conquests of the eastern Baltic tribal lands, the Order (as well as the other ruling parties) allocated fiefs and real estate to both native vassals and migrants in exchange for the payment of taxes and tithes, as well as military and economic services.[26] However, in contrast to the episcopates, who were more reliant on vassals for managing their territories, the Order's grants in both Livonia and Prussia typically involved small parcels of land.[27] In both regions the Order incorporated native forms of territorial organization and in this way, particularly in Livonia, the native organization of the landscape was, in part, retained. At the same time, land divisions used in the West were introduced, particularly the *Hufe* or *mansus*, with the *Hake*, *uncus* and *aratrum* all defining units of ploughland (between 8 and 12 hectares). Despite the varied subdivision of its administrative districts, the Order's approach to territorial management was cohesive and, in the case of planned settlements, land allocation was consistently uniform.[28]

In Livonia migrants came to be largely clustered in a small number of towns. These urban colonies were organized following templates established by a number of leading cities in the empire. The Lübeck Law, which was used in Danish Estonia, formed the basis of the Riga Law, which was used in the rest of Livonia.[29] Of the nineteen towns founded here up to the mid-sixteenth century, ten were located on the Order's territory and all originated alongside castles, with the exception of Riga.[30] A small number of native strongholds also continued to be occupied into the fourteenth century, reflecting the delegation of authority to native vassals. There was no settlement of the countryside by immigrant peasants and knights, most probably due to the prodigious costs of travelling across the Baltic (compared to Prussia, which was easier to reach), as well as the fact that much of the native population across Livonia remained intact and would grow in size over the fourteenth and fifteenth centuries.

In Prussia, the establishment of new settlements by migrating German peasants began in earnest in the 1280s and would continue into the later fifteenth century. This was most intensive in the Kulmerland, the region of the Lower Vistula and Ermland, while further east this process of 'colonization' intensified from the mid-fourteenth century. Initially, the majority of settlers came from Lower Saxony, North Rhine-Westphalia, Central Germany and Holland, while later generations born within Prussia would then become the dominant migrant group.[31] In the borderland that stretched from Masovia in the south through to the Memelland in the north, migrant settlements remained limited until the later fifteenth and sixteenth centuries, when they would include German, Polish and Lithuanian settlers.[32] In Prussia, the Order developed its own Kulm Law (Lat. *Ius Culmense*), derived from the Magdeburg Law. This was formulated in 1233, reissued in 1251 and granted to the majority of the 96 towns established there, of which the Order ruled over 72. These settlements were associated with the economic development of the landscape and some became very affluent communities, sponsoring the construction of their own churches.

The basic unit of property defined in the Kulm Law was the *mansus* (consisting of around 16.8 hectares), adopted from Flemish land divisions used in Silesia, which in turn had derived from earlier Carolingian designations of farmland. In addition to dealing with monetary regulations, military obligations and hereditary rights, the Kulm Law designated access to resources. It specified the Order's ownership of lakes and rivers, while granting fishing and milling rights to settlers. It also stated that the right shoulder of any game animal should be handed over to the Order, with the exception of beavers, which belonged to the brethren. Stipulated taxes consisted of a tithe of a measure of wheat and rye, and an annual tax of one-half mark per *Hufe* (interchangeable with Lat. *mansus* and Ger. *Hube*). Settlements were entrusted with an area ranging from 20 to over 100 *mansi*, with an average of 50–60 (roughly 840–1,000 hectares).[33]

The majority of towns on the Order's lands were established between the 1320s and 1350s, with more being founded in the first half of the fifteenth century. The Lübeck Law, which provided more autonomy, was granted to only seven towns, although it had already been adopted in Pomerelia before its annexation by the Order.[34] Nonetheless, the seizure of this duchy and its subdivision into commanderies prompted the construction of several castles and the proliferation of settlements organized under German laws, as well as the rebuilding and expansion of Danzig, which had been partly destroyed by the Order's army in November 1308.

Some native people migrated to the new towns in Livonia and Prussia. The majority, however, lived in rural settlements where they maintained their language and customs. Pre-Christian religious practices also endured longer in the countryside across large parts of Livonia and in Prussia, particularly in Samland. Part of the population was declared greater and lesser free (Ger. *grosse und kleine freie*) and a small group was able to enter the knightly class, while the majority were defined as peasants. In Prussia these were legally segregated, with native settlements governed by their own law (Lat. *Iura Prutenorum*) with relatively unfavourable conditions.[35] Only from the end of the fourteenth century were native Prussian peasants permitted to relocate to settlements organized under the Kulm Law.[36] Despite these levels of cultural segregation, Prussian and Livonian peasants were engaged in the construction of fortifications, provided military service and formed part of castle households. By the start of the fifteenth century the Prussian population probably numbered around 100,000 people, particularly in the interior and eastern parts of the province. This is reflected in the high number of toponyms containing native Prussian elements. But by the sixteenth century these toponyms stopped being used, reflecting the assimilation of the surviving native communities into the German and Polish population. This was the final stage in the disappearance of native Prussian language and culture.[37] The annexation of Pomerelia brought an additional 85,000 people under the Order's rule by the mid-fourteenth century:

most were Polish and Kashubian, with a smaller number of German speakers, particularly in Danzig.[38] Nonetheless, over time all inhabitants in the Order's extended Prussian province came to be regarded as 'Prussians' irrespective of what language they spoke.[39] In Livonia the population grew from an estimated 350–380,000 in the early thirteenth century to around 650–700,000 by the mid-sixteenth century.[40]

The relationship between the Order and its towns was one of overlord and subject, although the largest urban centres would become powerful in their own right. The Order oversaw the appointment of town councillors and controlled the defence, judicial and economic functions of these urban centres. The merchants of the leading Hanseatic towns in Prussia worked closely with the Order,[41] but in Livonia, when the Order acquired the holdings of the Sword Brothers, relations with the townspeople of Riga deteriorated. Despite this, Riga represented the Order's principal power centre in Livonia, with some sixty brothers documented in the convent there by the end of the thirteenth century, a number that had dropped to thirteen by 1442.[42] Reval (Est. Tallinn), governed by the Order from the mid-fourteenth century, also proved to be a problematic 'military partner'.[43] While the western Prussian towns were able to effectively organize themselves to challenge the Order's rule in 1440, with the exception of Riga, which came into conflict with the Order at various intervals through to the end of the fifteenth century, the Livonian towns generally supported the brethren.[44]

The Order's Economy and Trade

Following its territorial acquisitions in the Baltic, the Order's wealth derived from diverse revenue sources, including the tithe of a measure of wheat and rye from each *Hufe*, taxes, house taxes on individual buildings in towns, the taxation of various trades, milling and brewing, profits from mining, especially salt, the sale of amber (over which the Order had a monopoly), tolls on lake and river traffic, court fines, inheritance taxes, the auctioning of offices, licences for trapping and fishing, produce from the Order's estates, particularly grain, and the sale of war booty, as well as income from the Order's supporters and lands in its bailiwicks. The Order also produced its own coinage in both Prussia and Livonia: bracteates and larger, double-sided coins. The earliest *pfennig* coins produced from 1240 until 1260 were silver and were decorated with a range of images reflecting the Order's crusading ideology. Following the monetary reforms of Grand Master Winrich of Kniprode, three larger coin types were produced in the later decades of the fourteenth century – the *hälbing*, *schilling* and *vierling* – and in 1394 the Danzig mint struck gold coins. All of these displayed the grand master's shield and the Order's cross. The Order's Livonian branch produced its own coins separately, although without the grand master's eagle on its shields.

Taxes and tithes were typically paid in grain, which required the construction of substantial storage facilities and provided the Order with its most important commodity for export. The production and trade of grain defined the economies of both Livonia and Prussia, although it was far more developed in the latter.[45] The reason for this may be in the intensive rural settlement by migrants in Prussia, which saw the introduction of heavier ploughs and the expansion of cultivated land, while the agrarian practices of the native population in Livonia did not change until the fifteenth and sixteenth centuries, when the introduction of serfdom, the restructuring of the manorial economy and the reduction in the number of local vassals exercising power corresponds to an intensification in grain production.[46] In Prussia, the Order also developed specialized economies from abundant timber, fishing and amber resources. This saw the creation of districts specializing in forestry and fishing (Ger. *Fischämter*), as well as the office of amber master (Ger. *Bernsteinmeister*). Based at the castle in Lochstedt, he was responsible for the collection of this fossilized resin from the Sambian coastline, a luxury material that was often transformed into religious objects, particularly rosaries. Alongside timber, wax, honey and furs were procured from the Order's wooded districts. Specialized farms (Ger. *Vorwerke*) were also introduced, with 212 documented on the Order's Prussian lands by the start of the fifteenth century.[47] The Order was also one of the most important breeders of horses in late medieval Europe. An estimated 16,000 horses could be found in the castles, stud farms and estates of the Order in Prussia alone by the end of the fourteenth century, and a similar equestrian culture existed in Livonia.[48]

The Order became involved in trade from the very onset of its involvement in the Baltic, and the establishment of towns alongside its castles opened up the market for German traders and contributed to the rise of the Hanse. This was a confederation of largely German towns that came to dominate the maritime trade routes in late medieval Northern Europe. During the thirteenth century the principal centre of trade had been Visby on Gotland, which benefited significantly from the war economy generated by the crusades in the Baltic. At this time individual merchants or groups of merchants directed trading enterprises, but by the

Teutonic Order silver *schilling* of Winrich of Kniprode (1351–82).

mid-fourteenth century trade came to be dominated by a coalition of German towns and mercantile outposts, organized by Lübeck, which had steadily sapped Visby's influence in Baltic trade.

The Order benefited from having a number of towns with membership of the Hanse within its Prussian and Livonian lands, and Hanseatic merchants relied on access to Danzig, Elbing and Thorn for access to the Prussian market, Riga for Livonia, and Reval and Dorpat for the Rus' market. Hanseatic cities were also major recipients of the grain shipped from the Order's lands, especially from Prussia. For a time, the grand master was considered a member of the Hanseatic assembly, an exceptional position as all other members represented merchant communities of towns. He not only assumed a mediating role between Hanseatic merchants and European rulers, but could also take executive decisions on behalf of the coalition, as was the case with the Order's assault on Gotland, an action which had also been pushed for by the towns of Danzig and Marienburg. The Order's trade in Prussia was organized by the grand quartermaster (Ger. *Grossschäffer*) and his agents in Marienburg and Königsberg, while in Livonia it was supervised by the master and organized by lesser officials.[49] As a result of the revenues from its estates and its involvement in international trade, the Order became extremely wealthy. This enabled it to fund substantial building works, particularly from the late thirteenth century to the mid-fourteenth, when the largest buildings in late medieval Prussia and Livonia were constructed at the heart of the Order's political landscapes: the brethren's fortified convents.

SIX

Power and Faith: The Teutonic Order's Fortified Convents

Before becoming actively involved in the crusading frontier Baltic from the 1230s, the Teutonic Order had limited experience of castle building in the Levant and in
Transylvania. In Prussia, where there was no suitable building
stone, only large boulders – glacial erratics – scattered around
the landscape, the Order emulated the design of timber and
earthen strongholds it encountered and had experienced in
neighbouring regions, particularly Masovia. These strongholds
were referred to as *castra*, later translated as castles. Their principal buildings consisted of timber towers built on lower levels
of stone erratics, situated on top of earthen mounds or hills that
were fenced off with palisades and protected with additional
ramparts and towers. In Livonia, which had abundant limestone
and dolomite, but no native tradition of using mortared masonry,
a number of castles were built from stone in the decades before
the Order's involvement in the region. These early forms were
single buildings within or attached to a fortified enclosure, which
included a chapel. In 1237 the Order inherited a large number
of strongholds built by the Sword Brothers, of which six were
already masonry structures: Riga, Ascheraden (Latv. Aizkraukle),
Segewold (Latv. Sigulda), Wenden (Latv. Cēsis), Fellin (Est.
Viljandi) and Reval (Est. Tallinn); the last of these would be
handed back to the Danish king the following year. Between
the 1230s and the 1280s the Order's castles in both Prussia and

Livonia (as in the Levant and Transylvania) were irregular in design, often reflecting the constraints of local topography.

Conventual Castles

In the last two decades of the thirteenth century a new type of castle form became adopted by the Order for its principal command centres in the Baltic. This would later be referred to by scholars as conventual or claustral (that is, cloistered) castles (Ger. *Konventsburgen*), and typified the majority of the Order's rebuilt convents in the eastern Baltic.[1] These fortified convents reflected the Order's identity as a religious corporation, but more importantly as a sovereign territorial power, given that they were solely built on its lands in Prussia and Livonia.[2] The Order also constructed numerous smaller fortifications, from timber, stone and brick or a combination of all three, and single-range buildings and tower houses continued to be built into the fifteenth century.[3] The terminology used for all these buildings in contemporary sources is vague and interchangeable, as elsewhere in Europe, with *castellum* and *castrum* (castle, fort, stronghold) employed alongside *domus* and *haus* (house). The scholarship on the Order's castles, especially in Prussia, is vast and begins in earnest from the late nineteenth century when these structures started to be recognized as worthy of preservation rather than simply quarries for building materials, which had resulted in a number being partially or completely dismantled.[4] German antiquarians and conservationists documented many of these castles in detail; after several were damaged during the Second World War, from the 1950s onwards more systematic investigations by Polish, Latvian, Estonian, Lithuanian and Russian archaeologists, architectural historians and art historians began to be conducted, which have continued into the present day. The written record for these castles is best preserved for those in late medieval Prussia and remains limited for Livonia,[5] while many remain poorly understood from an archaeological perspective, not least of all those that have continued to be occupied and modified into the modern era.

Between the mid-thirteenth century and the early fifteenth, more than 120 castles were constructed in Prussia, excluding urban fortifications and the smallest fortified structures. The majority lie in the modern Polish part of former Prussia, where 60 of the Order's castles are documented; 28 of the Order's castles are known in the Kaliningrad Oblast and a smaller number were constructed in the borderland with Samogitia and Lithuania. Of all of these, 34 functioned as convents, although some only held this status for a short period. In Livonia the Order constructed at least 85 castles (68 known in Latvia and 17 in Estonia), of which a dozen functioned as convents. The Order's fortified architecture influenced the construction of castles of its neighbouring bishops and cathedral chapters. This was more so in Prussia than in Livonia, although the castle of Arensburg (Est. Kuressaare) on the island of Ösel (Est. Saaremaa) probably represents the most faithful replication of the conventual form, at least externally.

Building Conventual Castles

The origins of the conventual castle design continue to be debated. Suggestions have included the influence of monastic design, southern Italian architecture, Saxon construction techniques, Danish fortified camps and quadrangular castles in the Levant and Holy Roman Empire, as well as the masonry castles built by the Sword Brothers.[6] The Order's conventual castles were certainly reminiscent of cloistered monasteries, but their chapels or churches were usually contained within the rectilinear form of one range, rather than forming the organizational point and centrepiece of the claustral complex.[7] The use of brick, on the other hand, can be connected more convincingly with the Cistercians and Dominicans.[8] While most scholarly interest has focused on Prussia, it is possible the conventual form was first developed in Livonia, where it is evident from around the same time: the last two decades of the thirteenth century. In fact, searches for 'the first convent' may be misguided, since the decision to standardize conventual design must have been deliberated and agreed upon by the Order's governing body and then implemented in both regions.

The construction of brick and stone castles often meant the dismantling and levelling of earlier timber and earthen strongholds, although many castles were also built on fresh 'green field' sites, which were levelled in preparation. Trenches would be dug and filled with glacial erratics, which in turn provided a stable and waterproof foundation for the brick walls constructed above. Where soils were waterlogged, timber piles would be driven in first to support the stone foundations. The brick walls constructed on top typically consisted of a double row filled in with rubble, stones and mortar, although there are also instances of solid rows of brick.[9] These walls followed the form of the earlier earthworks, creating a new perimeter wall, which in some cases was irregular. Then a single brick range or building would be added to one side with a refectory, and a chapel located on its upper storey. Following this additional ranges would be added, which eventually formed the principal conventual building, later called the upper or high castle, or *Konventhaus* in the scholarly literature. This was typically situated in a naturally defendable location, often on higher ground. In some instances, cellar walls would be constructed at ground level around a courtyard, the surface of which would then be artificially elevated with soil, resulting in recessed chambers.

Transitional forms would have included both timber and brick elements, and timber superstructures were often filled in with clay, or sometimes brick. At Osterode, for example, the timber castle was gradually replaced with brick from 1349 over a period of twenty years. In the last decades of the thirteenth century, bricks were laid using the Wendish (or Slavic) bond, but from the early fourteenth century, this was replaced with the Gothic bond. This relative architectural dating, verified by recent OSL (optically stimulated luminescence) dating of brick phases at Malbork castle, has been used to establish a chronology of brick building construction in Prussia.[10] Some castles produced their own bricks, while others had to buy them in from other brick yards.[11] In Prussia the earliest conventual castles were built from brick in the region of the Lower Vistula and Lagoon, which included the provincial headquarters Elbing and the later seat of the grand master at Marienburg, as well as the castles

Ruins of the castle at Papowo Biskupie, Poland (Bischöflich Papau, Prussia).

Castle at Gniew, Poland (Mewe, Prussia), the best preserved of the
Teutonic Order's conventual castles.

of Brandenburg (Rus. Ushakovo) and Lochstedt. Cistercian
influence may be evident in these early castles where the use
of straight, symmetrical towers is reminiscent of the churches
attached to abbeys in Brandenburg and western Pomerania.[12]
Around the same time, a group of regular castles was built in the
Kulmerland, the earliest of which included the conventual castle
largely built from glacial erratics at Papau (Pol. Papowo Biskupie).[13]
In Livonia the earliest conventual castle appears to be Fellin,

where the regular convent building (47 by 45 metres) was constructed in the late thirteenth or early fourteenth century, with its
lower storey from stone, and upper storeys in brick.[14] By the first
half of the fourteenth century the claustral form was well developed. The last brick convent built in Prussia replaced the earlier
timber and earth stronghold at Ragnit (Rus. Neman) in the early
fifteenth century. The majority of conventual castles built by
the Order were rectangular with similar dimensions, ranging
from 40 metres by 52–66 metres,[15] clearly reflecting the adoption
of a standardized template. At the same time, variation in castle
size and form reflected the ambitions and agendas of various
agents involved in the building process. This included individual
commanders, who organized the construction process and dis-
tributed funds, while architects and masons would have advised
on practicalities.[16]

The Organization of Conventual Space

The conventual castle consisted of the enclosed upper castle,
and one or more connected outer wards (Ger. *Vorburgen*) with
additional buildings, all of which were enclosed by walls and
moats and connected with bridges. Some moats were dry, but
many were linked to rivers, lakes or canals. The upper castle
was composed of four regular ranges forming a quadrangle, with
towers projecting from each corner. One of these towers was
often larger and taller than the others, serving the function of a
keep. There was also typically an additional tower referred to as
a *Danzker*, which stood over the moat and was connected to the
upper castle by a covered walkway. It appears to have served as a
strongpoint, as well as containing latrines. The enclosed ranges
incorporated a set of integrated communal spaces on their first
floor: a dormitory, refectory, chapel or church and commander's
room, with kitchens and storage spaces in the floor below (which

Digital reconstruction of the Order's fortified convent at
Brandenburg, Prussia (Ushakovo, Russia).

may have included recessed cellars) and in the loft for regular,
short-term use – food, beverages and crockery. Additional spaces
may have accommodated a scriptorium and an infirmary. The
chapel was the focus of a convent's regular devotional activities and usually contained relics. Indeed, Gregory Leighton
has convincingly argued that the Order's castles, through their
relics and decorative schemes, contributed to the creation of a
new sacral landscape in the conquered territories of the eastern
Baltic.[17] Contrary to the widely held belief of earlier scholars,
the Order's castles did not contain dedicated spaces that served
as chapter houses. Instead, chapter meetings took place in refectories.[18] The most important spaces in the castle were heated
with stoves or hypocaust systems, which necessitated the use of
composite structures for the floors and walls, and these are documented in the Order's convents in both Prussia and Livonia.[19]

The upper castle buildings were enclosed by a moat, often separated from the castle building by a terrace referred to as a *parcham*
or *Zwinger*, some 6 to 10 metres wide.[20] It was most likely built to
provide further stability for the upper castle, but the terrace was

sometimes utilized for gardens or even tournaments, or bear and wild boar baiting, as well as for military purposes. Later on, farm buildings and commanders' residences were also built here.[21] The external wall of the outer ward typically reinforced the side of the moat. The inner ward or courtyard was surrounded by open arcades, reminiscent of a monastic cloister, and often contained a well. The number of outer wards and their size varied between castles and depended on their function, which typically consisted of storage areas, especially granaries and stables, as well as workshops, smithies, breweries and gardens. These functioned as centres of production for local consumption and trade.[22]

Larger castles had additional buildings. The most expansive was Marienburg, with two refectories, a separate residence for the grand master, a chancellery and two infirmaries: one in the first outer ward (later called the 'Middle Castle') and one in the second outer ward (later called the 'Lower Castle').[23] The former was reserved for the convent's brethren, but also functioned as accommodation during meetings of the Order's general chapter. The latter was used by the castle's household, soldiers, guests and pilgrims. Marienburg housed the second largest number of brethren in Prussia after Königsberg; in the early decades of the

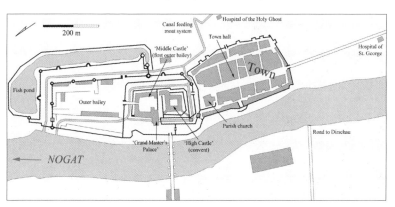

Marienburg, Prussia (Malbork, Poland), castle and town, at the end of the 14th century.

Aerial view from the east of the castle at Malbork, Poland
(Marienburg, Prussia).

fourteenth century 45 are noted and, during a siege, the fortified complex could accommodate 3,500–4,000 individuals engaged in its defence.[24]

Decoration

The Order's castles would have been decorated with imagery referencing the brethren's identity, heritage, devotion and crusading ethos. Very little of this has survived, and what has is known largely from a small number of Prussian castles, represented by extant or previously documented fragments of wall paintings, sculptures and portable objects, supplemented by material recovered during archaeological excavations. Written sources also indicate how certain spaces were furnished. The most important convents, which served as the residences of the Order's major officials, would have been impressively decorated, with the grand master's residence (later called a palace, but at the time referred to simply as *domus* or *meysters gemach*) in Malbork and the Livonian master's chamber in Cēsis representing the best-preserved examples of the level of luxury enjoyed by the Order's leadership. But glimpses are also visible in some of the other major convents. Excavations in the northern part of the outer ward at the castle in Elbląg, for example, recovered fragments of ceramic frieze tiles used in tracery. These were reminiscent of southern German styles from the 1320s and '30s, and most probably decorated the residence of the Prussian master in the early fourteenth century. Some of these architectural elements, such as vaulting ribs, were painted in polychrome.[25] In the late fifteenth and early sixteenth centuries, glazed tile stoves became popular in the towns of the Baltic Sea region. This is particularly evident from excavations of the Order's Livonian castles, where numerous stove tile fragments have been recovered, indicating the opulence of its major houses.[26] Although the grand master's

court in Marienburg in the late fourteenth century and the fifteenth has often been compared to a secular courtly residence,
the architecture and decoration of the grand master's residence
is closer to that of the Cistercians and mendicants, reflecting
adherence to the Order's principles.[27]

Heraldry

With an emphasis on recruitment from the imperial aristocracy
in the fourteenth and fifteenth centuries, the Order's castles began
to incorporate heraldic decoration reflecting the lineages of its
highest officials. The most important belonged to the grand masters, who had their coats of arms painted on the walls of castles
and churches, and carved on their funerary monuments. Ulrich
of Jungingen's family arms emblazoned the church in Juditten
in Samland (c. 1393–6), the western wing of the castle at Ragnit
(c. 1404–7) and the grand master's residence in Marienburg,
painted during the reign of his brother Konrad in 1403.[28] This
was a means of documenting his career within the Order, as he
progressed from advocate of Samland to marshal in 1404, and
finally to grand master in 1407.[29] In the last decade of the fourteenth century, the refectory ('chapter house') in the upper castle
of Marienburg was decorated with images of past grand masters,
emphasizing the heritage of the Order's rule in Prussia. The paintings in the commander's quarters at Lochstedt castle at the end
of the fourteenth century were decorated with figures of the 'Nine
Heroes', which included three models of Christian knightly
virtue: King Arthur, Charlemagne and Godfrey of Bouillon. On
another wall were knights of the Teutonic Order with banners
and arms, and figures of the grand commander, grand marshal,
grand hospitaller and grand quartermaster.[30] These are rare sur-
vivals, and it is likely that all of the Order's convents would have
been decorated in similar ways.

Bearing of the Teutonic Order's grand master depicted in the armorial
book of Ulrich Rösch, the abbot of St Gallen, c. 1463–91.

Religious imagery

A diverse range of Marian imagery was produced within medieval Livonia and Prussia.[31] Mary was the most important patron of the Order, protecting and legitimizing its authority. In this respect she was often presented as the Queen of Heaven on wall paintings and sculptures within the Order's convents.[32] Chapels would have been furnished with painted wooden sculptures, such as the enthroned Virgin and Child in the church in Gruta, dating to the third quarter of the thirteenth century and probably intended for the chapel of the castle in Roggenhausen (Pol. Rogóźno).[33] But the most striking example could be found at Marienburg, which was itself 'Mary's castle'. Here, an 8-metre-tall polychrome sculpture of artificial stone depicting the crowned Virgin and Child stood outside the eastern end of the chapel, set up during the extension of the upper castle's north range in 1331–44.[34] The figure, decorated in mosaic tiles about 1380, would have been visible from some distance to anyone approaching the castle from the east. The chapel itself would have been extensively decorated with Marian imagery, little of which has survived; a wall painting showing a brother of the Order kneeling before the enthroned Virgin and Child is a rare piece from the fourteenth century, and may be a votive image or epitaph of the murdered Grand Master Werner of Orseln.[35]

The Great Refectory in Marienburg's 'Middle Castle' was decorated with a scene of the Coronation of the Virgin, and the 'chamber of the grand master's companions' in the grand master's residence contains a scene with a knight kneeling before the Virgin. This theme of supplication was popular and survives on a reliquary commissioned by the commander of Elbing in 1388, which includes St Barbara in the vignette. It is also repeated in the portable *Schreinmadonnas* on which Teutonic brethren and their supporters were depicted under the Virgin's protective robe.

Restored Virgin and Child at the eastern end of the upper castle's church (initially chapel) in Malbork, Poland (Marienburg, Prussia).

The meaning of these images has been extensively debated, and given the close identification between Mary and the Teutonic Order it is difficult to untangle the religious and apotropaic functions of Marian art from its use as a political and corporate emblem.[36] Nonetheless, the devotional importance of Mary is underlined by her central role in the Order's liturgy.[37]

Partly restored in the 1880s, the 'golden gate' into the Church of the Blessed Virgin Mary is the best-known example of a decorated chapel entrance from the Order's convents, still largely intact in the upper castle in Marienburg.[38] Most likely reflecting an influence from the masons' workshop at Magdeburg, the moulded doorway stands at almost 4 metres, overlooked by a keystone on the vaulting above where Christ in judgement is represented within a mandorla. Its archivolt is decorated with grape vines, acanthus leaves and hybrid animals running up each side of the arch, all covered in polychrome and gold leaf. On the left side a siren-bird hybrid, a pig with oak leaves and acorns and a centaur emerge from the carved foliage; on the right a siren, locust and dragon are represented. Flanking the main archway are figures of *Ecclesia* – the Church Triumphant – and *Synagoga* with her characteristic blindfold, representing the inability to see the truth of Christ within the Jewish faith, and each leading figures of the wise and foolish maidens respectively. The use of monstrous hybrids and symbolic animals was widespread in the church decoration of the Order's convents: a fragment from Brandenburg bears a lion, and one from Lochstedt a dragon.[39] These are typically interpreted as didactic and apotropaic devices. On the 'golden gate', the hybrid resembling a hoofed lion carrying

The 'golden gate' in Malbork castle, Poland (Marienburg, Prussia).

a shield with a cross has been interpreted as representing the desire to enter the church beyond – the earthly incarnation of paradise.

While the iconographic programme has been interpreted as the Church under attack from Evil, the latter represented by the hybrids, here the viewers would be reminded of the Order's enduring struggle against pagans. A popular motif on chapel portals representing the evangelizing agenda of the Baltic Church was the apostolic college, which also symbolized the Church Triumphant.[40] More explicitly military representations, which have been interpreted as reflecting the Order's crusading mission in the Baltic, include a moulded brick tympanum from Birgelau castle (Pol. Bierzgłowo), dated about 1270–80, which shows a brother-knight mounted on a horse flanked by two Prussian warriors, one standing upright interpreted as an ally of the Order (presumably a Christian convert) and another submissive, representing the defeated pagan enemy. The rider's placement in a mandorla and the positioning of his sword and shield have been interpreted as referencing the figure of Christ the rider (Revelation 19:11). The accompanying inscription above may have also fulfilled an apotropaic function, reinforcing the notion of the Order's castles as beacons of sanctity in the dark pagan world.[41] The Great Refectory in Marienburg was decorated with scenes interpreted as the crusade against Prussian pagans; the southern wall was decorated with three painted bands depicting the Order's armies, while a column capital from elsewhere in the castle, dating to the first quarter of the fourteenth century, is carved with figures interpreted as the brethren fighting pagan Lithuanians. A biblical representation of the struggle against paganism could be seen in a wall painting at Lochstedt castle showing the archangel Michael as a crusader slaying the apocalyptic dragon, symbolic of the Order's righteous war against paganism and its inevitable outcome.[42]

Reproduction of
a wall painting at
Lochstedt (Rus.
Pavlovo) castle
showing the
archangel Michael
as crusader.

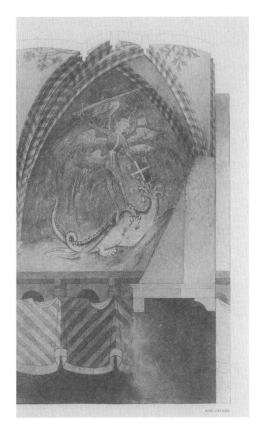

Directly below Marienburg's conventual church, the iconographic programme on the north and south portals of the chapel
of St Anne, constructed from artificial stone and dated to about
1340, contained well-established motifs: the coronation of the
Virgin and the seven wise and foolish maidens, the latter being
led into a mouth of hell. On the south tympanum the representation of the finding of the True Cross provided a direct
reference to Jerusalem.[43] Such references to the Holy Land reinforced links with the Order's heritage and original mission.

Castle Functions

The architectural historian Christofer Herrmann has described conventual castles as the perfect architectural synthesis of power and faith.[44] Each one was the principal centre of power within its district, where the administration of territory and judicial authority was exercised, taxes were collected and stored, and military resources were organized. The placement of the convent building on a raised earthen platform, segregated by one or more moats and walls, would have reinforced a sense of exclusivity. Its geometric design may also have been understood as a visible expression of order and perfection. Almost all the Order's convents were located next to planned or reorganized towns and shared an integrated defensive perimeter, although the castles dominated the skylines and were segregated from towns with their own walls and moats, visually reinforcing the Order's overlordship. This was particularly clear in Danzig (Pol. Gdańsk), where a substantial moat separated the castle's outer wards from the town on its northern, eastern and western sides, while the Motława river formed a natural barrier on the southern side of the complex. While serving defensive needs, this also created a visible sense of segregation and domination.

The brethren's identity as *Milites Christi* and their ability to enforce their governance through force would have been clearly legible in the convent's architecture, but with thick walls, corner and projecting towers, and easily defended connections between the upper castles and outer baileys, these structures were also constructed to be defendable. In the last decades of the fourteenth century, several castles began to be upgraded with additional towers and heightened walls, as part of a general investment by the Order in fortifications. In response to the increasing use of firearms and artillery, features such as bastions, gun loops and cannon embrasures also began to be added in the fifteenth century. After

1410, however, innovative castle building was largely carried out
by the Order's Livonian branch, which constructed structures
with substantial round corner towers as a response to artillery,
increasing their resistance to cannon while enhancing the effectiveness of defensive fire, and expanded inner courtyards with
new accommodation to house mercenary garrisons.[45]

The Order's convents also functioned as working military
centres, concentrating the production, maintenance and storage
of arms and armour, providing regular martial training and serving
as mustering points. The Order's armies were organized centrally
within each commandery and largely based on the obligations of
local townspeople, knights and other tenants to provide military
service. Alongside workshops for blacksmiths and armourers,
each convent had a space for storing weapons. Inventories of arms
in castle stores from the mid-fourteenth and fifteenth centuries
reveal that weapons and armour were stockpiled within the
Order's most strategically important castles, particularly in the
Kulmerland and at Marienburg, in preparation for warfare with
Poland.[46] Between 1364 and 1409 some 600,000 arrows were
stored in the Order's Prussian castles, of which 24,000 were kept
in Marienburg, as well as over a third of all armour held by the
Order in Prussia.[47] By the end of the fifteenth century crossbows
were becoming replaced by handheld firearms, and hook-guns
and matchlocks routinely feature in the inventories of the Order's
castles in the early sixteenth century.[48] Alongside smithies and
crossbow workshops, outer wards accommodated a range of additional manufacturing activities for both the needs of the convent
and external markets. There would also be spaces for gardens and
livestock, in particular stables for horses.

The increasingly complex governance of territory required
the establishment of smaller residences, essentially manors, which
were delegated to the Order's lesser officials. These were subordinated to the commanders whose districts they lay in, or at times

directly to the grand master, and took a variety of forms, reflecting their function within the Order's strategic management of its territories. Some were fortified, others were not, and they would be manned by one or two brethren with additional support staff. In the lengthy borderland of East Prussia, which was regularly targeted by Lithuanian armies in the fourteenth century, key military outposts consisted of single buildings attached to walled enclosures built from brick and stone. These could withstand raids better than timber and earth structures, providing shelter for local settlers and serving as mustering points.[49] These smaller residences often began as a *Wildhaus*, fulfilling both military and economic roles within the 'Great Wilderness'. Where it was not possible to build a masonry structure, other defensive measures were taken. The construction of the castle of Lyck (Pol. Ełk) on the southeastern edge of Balga's commandery at the start of the fifteenth century, first mentioned as a *Wildhaus*, began as a timber tower surrounded by a moat on three sides and palisades on the edge of an island situated between two lakes. The location was clearly intended to be defensive, and to provide shelter for local settlers who were encouraged to establish themselves nearby. The castle was soon upgraded to the residence of a procurator with the intention to exploit the resources of the surrounding woodlands, and would eventually be replaced in brick. The nearby settlement was granted privileges in 1425 and redefined as a town in 1440, although migrants would not arrive in the vicinity in large numbers before the sixteenth century; this protracted process of settlement reflected the changing stability of the frontier.[50]

In annexed Pomerelia, new castles were built in response to hostilities with Poland-Lithuania. They included the procurator's fortified residence in Ossiek (Pol. Osiek), which was constructed on a small island in a lake at the end of the fourteenth century or the start of the fifteenth. Its location was connected with one of the routes linking the Order's lands with the empire. The castle consisted of a single wing situated within an irregularly sided precinct that reflected the shape of the island. The complex was fitted with a chapel, kitchen, cellar, armoury, store, brewery and farm, and the procurator was responsible for managing farmland within the associated district: an inventory from 1428 lists 78 cattle, 465 pigs and 397 sheep.[51]

In Livonia the construction of smaller castles from the later thirteenth century also reflected the Order's strategic choices and provincial hierarchy. These were constructed in defensible locations in relation to routeways linking the Order's principal centres.[52] For example, the castle at Arrasch (Latv. Āraiši), first mentioned in 1410 but with archaeological evidence dating the earliest occupation to the late thirteenth century, was built on a raised peninsula on a lake off the road connecting Wenden with Riga. In southern Estonia, the castle at Karkus (Est. Karksi), constructed in the late thirteenth century on a 'greenfield site' protected by steep valleys, guarded the road connecting Fellin

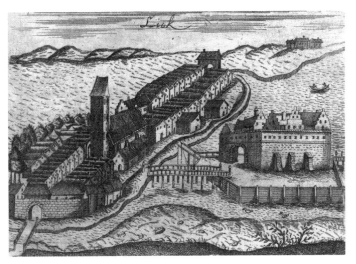

Woodcut showing the castle and town of Lyck in East Prussia (Ełk, Poland), 1684.

Reconstruction of the Teutonic Order's castle at Arrasch in Livonia (Āraiši, Latvia).

with Wenden and ultimately Riga – linking the Order's territories in northern and southern Livonia.[53] Karkus was subordinated to Fellin and Arrasch to Wenden, supporting the territorial management of their commanders. When the Order acquired the Duchy of Estonia in 1346, it rebuilt the strongholds of Reval, Wesenberg (Est. Rakvere) and Narwa (Est. Narva) as conventual castles, adopting the political landscape established by the Danish crown, and imposing its own subdivision of territory. At this point Narwa became the most important borderland castle for the Order's Livonian branch, while Weißenstein (Est. Paide), previously on the frontier with the Duchy of Estonia, retained its former importance within the Order's hierarchy.[54]

SEVEN

Crusading in the Wilderness: The Teutonic Order's Wars against Lithuania

Following the creation of the Catholic polities of Livonia and Prussia, the Teutonic Order began to lead regular military campaigns (or *Reysen* as they were called in Middle High German) against the Grand Duchy of Lithuania and the region of Samogitia. This region bordered with the Order's northeast Prussian and Curonian commanderies, and here the local nobility also exercised a certain level of independence from the grand dukes. In leading said campaigns, the brethren repackaged the crusading experience for Catholic nobles and provided ideal opportunities for young male aristocrats to 'earn their spurs'. Both of the Order's Baltic branches had faced Samogitian and Lithuanian armies in the thirteenth century, particularly from the 1260s, but following the final subjugation of the Prussian tribes in 1283, Peter of Dusburg wrote that the war with the Lithuanians began immediately thereafter.[1] That year the Prussian master Konrad of Thierberg attacked Lithuanian strongholds on the Nemunas (also Nemen or Memel) river, the start of a relentless series of campaigns, which were met with reprisals. Historians have typically laid the blame for the continuing war on the Order, which was intent on seizing Samogitia and uniting its Prussian and Livonian lands. At the same time, these wars were part of the Order's self-promotion as the defender of Christendom against pagans. The Lithuanian grand dukes were more interested in expanding their realms to the east, to

Rus' lands and the Black Sea, and their raids into Prussia and Livonia were not intended to capture territory.

Crusading in the Fourteenth Century

After a lull in the participation of foreign knights in the eastern Baltic for three decades, a group of German crusaders accompanied the Order's armies in eastern Prussia to the Lithuanian strongholds of Grodno (Lith. Gardinas) and Pograuda (Lith. Pagraudė) in 1305. More German knights followed in later years, eventually joined by English participants in the winter of 1328–9. They, in turn, were followed by knights from the Netherlands, northern France and northern Italy, then from Scotland, southern France and southern Italy. Within a few decades, knights from across Christendom were travelling to Prussia, even from as far away as Iberia, and Polish knights also participated for a time. Between 1305 and 1403 some three hundred campaigns into Samogitia and Lithuania were organized by the Order, intensifying in the period from 1360 to 1393, as the northeastern frontier of Latin Christendom became the predominant theatre for crusading.[2]

Some historians have argued that these were not crusades, but rather chivalric adventures for glory-seeking knights, not to mention an important source of revenue for the Order. Alan Murray, for example, described them as 'a relatively risk-free form of military tourism distinguished by little other than conventional piety'.[3] At the time a young knight's reputation was based on accruing experiences of service within a noble household, jousting, fighting in battles and, if the opportunity presented itself, going on crusade. In the fourteenth century the Order's *Reysen* provided an ideal opportunity to invest in reputation, and participation could even become a family tradition. But whether the spiritual dimension of campaigning with the brethren was nothing more than conventional piety remains debated. Earlier papal privileges, such as those issued by Pope Alexander IV in the late 1250s, allowing the Order's clerics the right to grant a crusading indulgence to all who had fulfilled their vow, continued to be used by the brethren into the fifteenth century. These had become formulaic prescriptions and surviving examples of 'the indulgence of the *Reyse*' described how crusading in the Baltic followed on directly from the Holy Land, and stated on the basis of several papal grants that the indulgence extended to those who came to Prussia and Livonia at their own expense, with true repentance, to fight against 'the heathen', as well as any Christians supporting them.[4] Proof of the indulgence could be obtained from the Order's officials in the form of a certificate, although only one example of this has survived. These were not the only indulgences issued by the Order, but those pertaining to fighting pagans were solely found in its branches actively involved in the war with Lithuania. In this respect the Order could launch its own 'crusades', without requiring explicit papal authorization for each campaign. Nonetheless, on at least one occasion – in 1386 – the pope issued an indulgence to all those who would aid the Order in their fight against pagans.

The expeditions would also begin on significant days associated with the Virgin Mary: the Feast of Our Lady of the Candles (2 February), the Feast of the Assumption (15 August) and the Birthday of the Virgin (8 September).[5] In this respect the Order tied the *Reysen* closely to the divine patron and sovereign of Prussia, emphasizing the penitential aspect of the campaigns. Armies would be led into battle by the Virgin; the banner emblazoned with her image and first referenced in the fourteenth century ranked among the highest in the Order. Throughout this time the Order's Prussian brethren were regularly referred to as *cruciferi* (crusaders) by their Catholic neighbours, while those participating in the campaigns were called *perigrini* (pilgrims), as well as the Order's 'guests'.[6] The résumé of Chaucer's knight included fighting Muslims in Iberia and North Africa and Turks in the Levant, as well as the Lithuanians, demonstrating that the Baltic frontier was, in the minds of contemporaries, one of the key fronts of Christendom. Indeed, the Order promoted itself as the principal defender of Latin Christendom against not only the pagan Lithuanians, but the schismatic Orthodox Rus'.[7]

The majority of *Reysen* took place across the eastern Prussian frontier. If these campaigns were cancelled, due to a mild or severely harsh winter making traversing through the wilderness difficult, knights would sometimes move on to Livonia hoping for a better chance to participate in the following season. In contrast, few armies crossed into Samogitia from the north in the fourteenth century. Instead, the Livonian brethren's attacks were focused on Pskov, a city state under the influence of the Lithuanian grand dukes. Russian Christians were variously por-trayed by the Order's chroniclers, but those from Pskov were considered the worst kind of schismatics, viable targets for cru-saders. From the mid-fourteenth century this labelling became increasingly commonly applied as the notion of Livonia as a frontier of 'true' Christendom became more pronounced. This, in turn, led to anti-German sentiment and a negative perception of Catholicism developing first in Pskov before filtering through into the broader body of Old Russian literature.[8] The *Reysen* were so established as an institution that even after the official conversion of Lithuania to Christianity in 1386/7 they did not diminish in popularity, and knights continued to flock to Prussia into the 1420s.[9] By this time, however, people were beginning to question why the Order was attacking neighbouring Catholic states and participation in the brethren's wars eventually ceased.

Organizing the *Reysen*

The majority of named participants were drawn from the upper and lower ranks of the knightly class, as well as from urban patrician families; only occasionally did rulers make the journey to the frontier. Many participants hailed from the Order's traditional bases of support within the Holy Roman Empire, particularly *ministeriales*, young knights who were legally unfree and bound to their liege lords, but who also commanded their own armed vassals. Yet the popularity of the *Reysen* with the English, a realm whose principal connection with the Order was commercial, and particularly with the port of Danzig (Pol. Gdańsk), points to a broader appeal.[10] English participants came to the Prussian frontier when the opportunity presented itself, particularly during interludes of peace in the Hundred Years' War, but some even undertook the journey in the midst of the Black Death. The English crown had even supported the Order with an annual pension, although this was paid erratically and the last time this happened was in 1401, under Henry iv.

Kinsmen regularly travelled together, as did extended noble households and those joined by ties of vassalage; the largest royal and ducal retinues numbered in their hundreds and, when added to the Order's forces, the armies could be substantial. For example, Henry, Duke of Lancaster (the maternal grandfather of the future Henry iv of England), was accompanied by a retinue of four hundred people in 1351–2, at least a thousand combatants were involved from the empire alone in the winter of 1354–5, while the Austrian prince Leopold iii brought 1,500 horses with him in 1371–2. Joining the Order's *Reysen* became a family tradition for some, with multiple generations making the journey and some even becoming regulars on the circuit. The majority of those who came to fight in Lithuania returned home after completing their service, but some lingered or travelled to join other campaigns.

For a few, Prussia and Livonia were just stopping points on much longer tours, often featuring a visit to the Holy Sepulchre in Jerusalem. Such journeys could last four or five years and only the wealthiest could afford to indulge in such extensive pilgrimages.

The expeditions were serious investments and the costs could be significant. With the return journey, most participants could expect to be away for four to five months. Those leading companies had to pay a daily sum to each member of their retinue: on average some 20 per cent of the expenses went on wages. Other expenditure included horses and saddles, clothes, raw cloth, dishes and other tableware, weapons, armour, provisions (in large quantities for sea voyages, for both men and animals), banners and liveries. There were also spiritual requirements such as the upkeep of a chaplain and the purchase of a portable altar. The wealthiest would bring their dogs and falcons, along with their handlers, and their companies became miniature courts on the move. Upfront loans were often required, and since it was safer to make the journey carrying as little cash as possible, once out in Prussia further loans were sought, which Hanseatic merchants, as well as the Order's representatives, were on hand to provide. Although as an ecclesiastical organization the Order was not permitted to charge interest on any loans, within its own lands the Order's coinage had to be used, and participants predictably lost out on exchange rates. Many knights returned heavily in debt, although few would be financially broken by the experience. These transactions were most often conducted in Bruges, which was the leading commercial hub in Western Christendom at the time and contained a substantial community of Prussian merchants, as well as the Order's own agents.

The knights who joined the Order's campaigns were expecting to be treated well and to replicate their courtly life as best as they could, with feasts, tournaments, opportunities to hunt in the forested borderlands, and all the ceremonial trappings of chivalric culture. The principal mustering point was Königsberg (Rus. Kaliningrad), where the Order's guests were lodged in hospices within the town. At one point the convent here housed the largest community of brethren in the Order's Baltic territories (some 67 brethren are associated with it in 1422), and also served as the seat of the Order's Prussian marshal, who led the campaigns into Lithuania. He would present the most distinguished guests with gifts, which included deer and even bison, procured from the 'Great Wilderness'. The marshal assigned brethren and free native Prussian subjects to look after each company, and those who required medical care would be sent to the Order's doctors, even to the grand master's own personal physician at times. The companies would set themselves up, creating a series of small, itinerant courts, and then wait for the campaigns to begin – sometimes for days, often weeks and perhaps even months. During this time the nobles gambled, played chess, exchanged gifts, visited brothels and entertained guests from other companies with lavish banquets, as well as the Order's officials, the local bishop and his canons. If the wait was going to be long, hunting

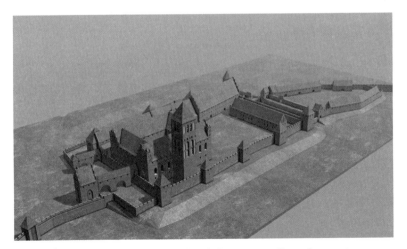

Digital reconstruction of the Order's fortified convent at Königsberg, Prussia (Kaliningrad, Russia).

expeditions would be organized, and some nobles brought falcons and hunting dogs in anticipation of this; others would be granted or loaned them by the Order. Although no tournaments were organized, companies would sometimes engage in informal war games with each other. In the last decades of the fourteenth century, a chivalric pageant known as the 'Table of Honour' was organized by the Order and presided over by the marshal or grand master. This lavish feast took place in the refectory of the Königsberg convent, where guests, organized by heralds, were seated by rank, speeches praised their deeds and the whole event would culminate in the ceremonial award of a badge for valour. Later, in 1415 at the papal Council of Constance, the representative of the Polish king argued this was a scandalous way for the Order to extract large sums of money from its guests.[11] However, this clearly provided an attractive chivalric element for the participants.

Some of the churches within the vicinity of Königsberg became popular with participants of the *Reysen*. This included the church of St Anthony and, in particular, the chapel of St George attached to the leper hospital in the southern suburb of Haberberg. St George was of course the quintessential crusader saint and an altar dedicated to him could also be found in the cathedral at Kneiphof, one of the towns that made up Königsberg. Foreign knights would visit the chapel in Haberberg to pray for a successful campaign before setting out to Lithuania, and also upon their return to thank the saint for protecting them. Several visitors made donations to the chapel and painted their heraldic emblems on boards hung inside. Beyond the suburbs, the most visited churches were St Katherine's in Arnau, some 10 kilometres along the Pregel river, east of Königsberg, and the Blessed Virgin's in Juditten, 7 kilometres to the west. Again, some visitors had their heraldic arms painted on the walls inside these two pilgrimage sites. In Juditten this included images of fully armoured knights alongside their coats of arms, among which could be found those of the Jungingen brothers, Konrad and Ulrich, who would both rise up the ranks to become the Order's grand masters. But the *Reysen* were above all memorialized in the cathedral, which was an essential part of the itinerary for all visitors at the start and end of their journey. Here, the walls of the nave were painted with the heraldic emblems of previous participants, as were the tombs of those who fell in battle against the pagans, with their arms painted on the cathedral's windows. Part of a wall painting in the cathedral from 1360, heavily modified during nineteenth-century restorations, represented pilgrims arriving in Prussia as crusaders.[12] During Mass the cathedral would have provided the ideal setting for sermons extolling the virtue of the righteous war to defend Christendom, and a place of reflection on victory and loss. Participants who died in the course of the expeditions could also be buried in the cathedral; the English knight Sir Geoffrey Scrope died in his early twenties in 1363 following a siege of a Lithuanian stronghold, and his companions arranged for his coat of arms to be included as a panel in one of the cathedral's stained-glass windows and on a slab in front of the altar. Crusaders could also be buried elsewhere within the Order's lands depending on their company's routes back, such as in St Mary's Church in Danzig.[13]

The 'Great Wilderness': Frontier between the Christian and Pagan Worlds

Once the call came, participants gathered and marched with the Order's army into the so-called 'Great Wilderness' (Ger. *Die Große Wildnis*). Contemporary chroniclers referred to this region in terms that were commonly used to describe the biblical wilderness,[14] and for the Order's guests this frontier was both a physical and spiritual desert, a fitting backdrop for the holy war against paganism. The Order's wars targeting southwestern Lithuania in the late thirteenth century depopulated this region, which would not see recolonization until the sixteenth century. The eastern Prussian frontier was marked by a series of castles, governed from the convents of Balga, Brandenburg (Rus. Ushakovo) and Königsberg. Dendrochronological dating of material from excavations at the Order's site in Sztynort (Ger. Steinort) indicated it was constructed about 1315,[15] while the castles at Angerburg (Pol. Węgorzewo), documented from 1335, and Johannisburg (Pol. Pisz), documented from 1346, may have had earlier foundations.[16] Together with Lötzen (Pol. Giżycko), they have often been interpreted as a defensive line guarding the passes across the Galindian lakelands,[17] perhaps even supported by a series of watch towers.[18] At the southern end of this line the procurator's castle at Eckersberg (Pol. Okartowo), situated on the road between two lakes, is documented about 1340. In the late 1360s and '70s Grand Master Winrich of Kniprode instigated the construction of castles at Rudwangen (Pol. Rydwągi), Bosemb (Pol. Boże), Weißenburg (Pol. Wyszembork) and Rhein (Pol. Ryn). Together with Rastenburg (Pol. Kętrzyn), established in earlier decades, and Bäslack (Pol. Bezławki), which may have been constructed from the third quarter of the fourteenth century,[19] they represented an additional defensive cluster marking the western edge of the 'Great Wilderness'.

The accompanying settlement took a long time to develop, and there was a general sense of insecurity, especially from the mid-fourteenth century. Some settlements were established only to vanish following Lithuanian incursions, best represented archaeologically by Alt-Wartenburg, located near Barczewko within the former centre of the Ermland episcopate. Excavations uncovered a destroyed town, which has been linked to the documented Lithuanian attack in the winter of 1354.[20] The town was one of several that had been founded in the early decades

Digital reconstruction of the Order's procurator's residence at
Rastenburg, Prussia (Kętrzyn, Poland).

of the fourteenth century; 10 kilometres to the south, the castle
and town of Allenstein would see significant investment from
the Ermland chapter. The destruction of castles also delayed the
development of a settlement pattern. Angerburg was destroyed
by a Lithuanian army in 1366 and would not be rebuilt until
more than three decades later and 2 kilometres away from the
original site, Eckersberg was destroyed in 1378, while the castle
at Goye, noted in 1384, is no longer mentioned in fifteenth-
century sources.[21] Most settlement in the southeastern Prussian
frontier before the mid-fifteenth century was focused around the
procurator's castle at Johannisburg. The Order's garrison here
saw major confrontations with the Lithuanians in the 1360s
and at one point the castle was besieged and the surviving garrison enslaved. The castle was rebuilt and in 1392 hosted the
Order's guests during a *Reyse* led by the Order's grand marshal.
The development of settlement would not begin here in earnest
until 1422.[22]

To the northeast, in the vicinity of Straduny, settlement would not develop until the 1470s and would only intensify from the sixteenth century. The northeastern frontier of Prussia was administered from the convent at Memel, situated on a fortified island, where finds of locally manufactured pottery and native jewellery, alongside grey ware and imported vessels, have been connected to the presence of native Catholic converts serving in the convent's household.[23] The town that developed alongside the castle was the target of regular destructive attacks by Samogitian armies.[24] As a result of its precarious frontier location, Memel was unable to become self-sufficient and had to import its major foodstuffs from across every border; even in the sixteenth century it was dependent on neighbouring Samogitia for its beef. Memel was also one of the mustering locations for armies to set off on *Reysen*, who would then travel along the Nemunas river. Most, however, would leave from Königsberg.

Reconstruction of the types of horses used by the Teutonic Order in eastern Prussia during the *Reysen*.

These armies then made their way to the Order's castle of Ragnit (Rus. Neman), which had been built in 1288 on the site of a destroyed native stronghold in the heart of the Prussian tribal territory of Scalovia. Within a few decades it housed a convent, but the castle remained largely a timber and earth fortification, one of a series of strongholds built by the Order throughout the fourteenth century along the river that cut into the heart of Lithuania. These were regularly attacked and damaged or destroyed by Lithuanian armies. In the 1380s and '90s the last castles were built on islands, and their names hark back to the strongholds of the earlier crusades – Marienwerder (Mary's island), Ritterswerder (Knight's island) and Gotteswerder (God's island) – with some of the foreign nobles who arrived at the frontier contributing to their construction. The castle of Georgenburg, surviving as earthworks broadly datable to the fourteenth century at Kalnénai in Jurbarkas, was destroyed by the Lithuanians in 1384 only to be rebuilt a few years later and finally burned again in 1403. Ragnit, holding out against numerous raids, would be the last of the Order's convents to be upgraded to brick, with construction work starting in 1397 and finishing twelve years later. In its final form it was the epitome of the Order's fortified monastic design: a perfect square measuring 59 metres on each side, with three ranges of service buildings lining an adjacent ward – the whole complex encircled by a moat and wall.[25] Its commanders governed a precarious territory populated by native communities, and even during its construction Ragnit had been attacked by Lithuanian armies with devastating consequences in 1402 and again the following year, then again in 1411, after the convent's completion.

Survival in the 'Great Wilderness' was about logistics, tailored to the appropriate season, and winter was the most popular time for campaigns, when the countless lakes, marshes and rivers were frozen and there was enough snow cover on the ground to provide traction for horses and men. In the summer, it was easier to travel by river and the Order provided its own fleet, otherwise participants had to rent additional boats. At this time, the marshes and lakes were particularly unpleasant, infested with swarms of biting insects. Substantial numbers of pack horses were required, especially in the winter as they were far better suited to the terrain than wagons, although sledges were also readily used. It is easy to imagine the larger convoys stretching over several kilometres. Provisions would always be at the top of the list, and had to be carefully planned out for the duration of a *Reyse*, which lasted from several days to a few weeks. With the exception of hunting for game, which was time-consuming and unpredictable, it was impossible to procure supplies once armies had passed the last settlements on the frontier.

The Politics of the *Reysen*

The Order's attacks steadily penetrated into the heart of the Lithuanian grand duchy. In 1288 the Prussian master Meinhard of Querfurt constructed the stronghold named Landshut, later Ragnit. Grand Duke Butigeidis attacked Samland in 1289 and began to fortify the Nemunas river. That year the Order built Tilsit castle on the same river and began to launch regular assaults into Lithuanian territory. Between 1294 and 1300 Ludwig of Liebenzell, the commander of Ragnit, led regular attacks against Samogitia, which continued into the following decade. In 1311 the Lithuanians attacked Ermland, reaching Pogesania and even the Kulmerland. The reign of Grand Duke Gediminas (1316–41) was marked by ongoing conflict with the Prussian brethren, but in 1322 a peace was agreed between the grand duchy and the Livonian brethren and episcopates. During the reign of the Polish king Casimir III (1333–70) there was peace between the Order and Poland, particularly after the signing of the Treaty of Kalisz in 1343, enabling the brethren to concentrate their military efforts on Lithuania. Conflict between the Order and Poland would not commence again until 1409, although the union of Poland and Lithuania brought Polish military resources to the defence of the grand duchy.[26]

The intervening years were marked with periods of regular warfare. In 1337 the German emperor Louis IV, who was a major supporter of the Order, granted the brethren dominion over any lands conquered in Samogitia and Lithuania, although this was more of a symbolic gesture. In February of the following year the Order fought the Lithuanians by the frozen Strėva river, a tributary of the Nemunas. The Lithuanians were soundly defeated and another peace was agreed with Gediminas, although attacks continued. Between 1362 and 1382 the Order's Prussian branch carried out over 50 campaigns into Lithuania, while its Livonian branch carried out 22 attacks over the borderlands. Lithuanian reprisals into eastern Prussia were particularly severe in 1376. Several Lithuanian grand dukes had contemplated or even actively promoted the Christianization of their realm, in order to place it under papal protection and halt the Order's assaults. This would be finally achieved in 1386 with the baptism of Jogaila, but the brethren did not stop their attacks. In fact, they intensified during the last decades of the fourteenth century, as the brethren also became involved in the civil war between Jogaila and his cousin Vytautas, who sought to keep Lithuania separate from Poland. This resulted in the Order and Vytautas's forces besieging Vilnius (unsuccessfully) in September 1390. Vytautas would eventually cede Samogitia to the brethren in October 1398. In 1401 Vytautas encouraged the Samogitians to rise up against the Order's rule, which resulted in further conflict until another peace was signed in 1404, confirming the Order's hold on the region. When a second Samogitian uprising began in May 1409, this would be the catalyst for the 'Great War' between the Order and Poland-Lithuania.

The End of the *Reysen*

In the 1390s the number of English and French knights travelling to Prussia was at its peak, at a time when Polish knights were fighting in the defence of Lithuanian lands against the Order's assaults. Then, in the summer of 1394, the numbers started to fall, marking a slow decline in attendance. The threat of the Ottoman Turks was drawing the attention of would-be crusaders to the eastern Balkans, as the Order's justification for attacks against a Catholic state was being questioned. A small number of knights came to Prussia in the early years of the fifteenth century, but the enthusiasm in some regions that traditionally supplied knights had clearly evaporated. English participants came individually in the years leading up to the outbreak of the 'Great War' between the Order and Poland-Lithuania in 1409. The Order had accused the Lithuanians of sham conversions to Catholicism and branded the Poles enemies of the faith for aiding heathens, not to mention the Tartars deployed in their armies, the 'true Saracens'.[27] The Order's argument was certainly compelling to its guest knights and some foreign observers, but English chroniclers were beginning to turn against the brethren, castigating them for attacking Jogaila, who had converted to Catholicism.[28] For English knights the revived war with France, as exemplified under the leadership of Henry v, superseded crusading as the paragon of chivalric activities.

It would not be until the Council of Constance, which commenced in 1414 and dragged on for three years, attended by clerics and delegates from across Christendom, that the Order's mandate to wage holy war against Lithuania was publicly challenged. Here, the most detailed defence of the Order's *raison d'être* was presented to the papal commission, reiterating the old arguments against Lithuania and Poland. From the Order's perspective, Christians who aided pagans were viable targets, as

clearly stated in their indulgence of the *Reyse*. The head of the
Polish delegation, Paweł Włodkowic, argued on legal grounds that
the Order's war and their intended occupation of Samogitia by
force was unjust, criticizing the conversion of infidels by force. A
group of recently baptised Samogitians was brought in to demonstrate the effectiveness of conversion under the Lithuanian-
Polish Union. Both sides presented themselves as defenders of
the Catholic faith against pagans and schismatics. In the end,
the newly appointed pope, Martin v, hesitated to sanction the
Order directly, but handed the responsibility for evangelizing
the Samogitians to Poland-Lithuania. The winter of 1422 saw the
final contingent of German knights make the journey with the
aim of participating in a *Reyse*. They arrived just as a defining peace
treaty had been concluded, with the Order finally renouncing
its rights to Samogitia. The treaty also officially demarcated the
border between eastern Prussia and Lithuania.

EIGHT

Defeat and Decline in the Fifteenth Century

In the late fourteenth century the Teutonic Order was experiencing an identity crisis. In 1386 Jogaila, the Grand Duke of Lithuania, was baptised, adopting the Polish name Władysław Jagiełło. A few days later Jagiełło married the Polish sovereign Jadwiga, daughter of the late king Louis I, and was crowned king of Poland and Lithuania. This political union, creating one of the most powerful states in late medieval Europe, now under the nominal protection of the Catholic Church, presented an existential challenge to the Order. Their military campaigns targeting Lithuania could no longer be justified as an ongoing holy war against paganism.[1] Increasing secular tendencies and a decline of interest in the religious life among the brethren were also evident, with falling standards noted in some of the Prussian convents in the first half of the fifteenth century.[2] Recruiting from the German aristocracy was becoming difficult, in part because the brethren's lifestyle was not proving attractive enough. By the start of the fifteenth century there were some 700 brother-knights, brother-sergeants and brother-priests in Prussia, and around 250 in Livonia. By 1437 the number in Prussia had decreased to below 400, by the middle of the century it was around 300 and finally by 1525 there were only 55 brethren remaining. This was also reflected in the Order's imperial bailiwicks, where membership fell by two-thirds over the course of the fifteenth century. As a result,

the Order was forced to increasingly rely on mercenaries to
garrison its castles.[3]

By the end of the fourteenth century the Order's finances
were still healthy and money was pouring into Marienburg's (Pol.
Malbork) treasury. But the next decade proved costly. In 1402 the
Order purchased the Neumark, and its military campaigns against
the Vitalien (or Victual) Brothers, which saw the pirates expelled
from their base in Gotland in 1398, was followed by the Order's
(contested) purchase of the island and its subsequent defence
against Queen Margaret of Denmark's army in 1404. The construction of the castles at Ragnit (Rus. Neman), Dirschau (Pol.
Tczew) and Bütow (Pol. Bytów) at this time also resulted in significant expenditure, and the ensuing war with Poland-Lithuania
and the reparations had a significant impact on the Order's
finances. Income sources from its Baltic commanderies and
European bailiwicks declined, although not as drastically as had
once been thought. Nonetheless, a major problem that endured
throughout the fifteenth century was the debasement of the
Order's currency, coupled with inflation, as grand masters reduced
the amount of silver in their coinage to mitigate their declining
finances. This, in turn, made the Order's own coinage less valuable. Towards the end of the fifteenth century Grand Master John
of Tieffen introduced new coins (*scoters*, later *groschen*), in an
attempt to improve the monetary standard, but fiscally the Order
was in long-term decline. The Order's financial crisis prompted
it to increase taxation, which contributed to undermining the
legitimacy of the brethren's rule in Prussia.[4]

The Order's hold over Samogitia continued to be disputed by
the Lithuanian duke and Polish king, and as a result its war with
Lithuania transformed into a secular conflict with the Polish-
Lithuanian union. Over the course of the fifteenth century the
Order's Prussian branch suffered a series of military defeats, with
Grunwald in 1410 often highlighted as a historical watershed,

and uprisings from its key towns, followed by a significant loss of territory and with it, income. For the Livonian brethren, the major military events after the conquest of Semigallia had been the war against the town of Riga in 1297–1330 and the Estonian uprising in 1343–5. There was small-scale conflict with Lithuania and Pskov and the suppression of the rebelling vassals of the Archbishop of Riga in 1395 after John of Wallenrode took over the office and joined the ranks of the Order. There was also a short clash with the coalition of the Bishop of Dorpat in 1396–7. Later the Livonian brethren became involved in the Lithuanian civil war (1432–8), a further war against Riga (1481–91) and a short-lived war against the Muscovite state (1501–3).

The Livonian masters began to act increasingly independently, edging away from Marienburg's centralized control. Yet the inherent weakness of multiple territorial powers in Livonia acting independently remained, despite the assembly of Livonian diets from 1420 onwards and attempts to rally the country together against the threat of Muscovy at the end of the fifteenth century. The Order's bailiwicks continued to play an important role in imperial politics, and the German master would come to the fore in the sixteenth century with the secularization of the Order's Prussian branch in 1525, and the surrender of the Livonian branch to Poland and subsequent secularization in 1561.

The Order's Wars with Poland-Lithuania

The Teutonic Order's foreign policy in the fifteenth century was dominated by a series of wars and peace treaties between its Prussian branch (primarily) and Poland-Lithuania. The origins of this conflict can be traced back to the Order's seizure of Pomerelia in 1308–9, which was temporarily resolved by the Treaty of Kalisz in 1343, resulting in six decades of relative peace between Poland and the Order. However, Poland's union with Lithuania changed everything. Throughout the fourteenth century the Order had been involved in a protracted war against Samogitia and the grand duchy. This had involved taking sides in the civil wars between competing Lithuanian dukes to further its territorial aspirations, conflicts which from 1386 began to directly involve Poland. As a result, the peace that had been established at Kalisz gradually disintegrated.

The decline in trade agreements between the Order and Lithuania from the mid-fourteenth century coincided with an intensification of attacks against the grand duchy. With the grand duchy's official adoption of Catholicism, a new agreement would give merchants from Vilnius and Polotsk access to Riga. Then, in January 1390, Vytautas (who had converted to Catholicism a few years before Jogaila) made a secret pact with the Order, agreeing to cede them a portion of Samogitia in exchange for a military alliance against Jogaila and his brother Skirgaila. Four months later, this was reaffirmed in a treaty signed in Königsberg by thirty Samogitian nobles who acknowledged Vytautas's lordship. In September the Order's army, accompanied by an English contingent led by Henry Bolingbroke (the future king Henry iv), stormed the walls of Vilnius along with a Lithuanian contingent, in an unlikely alliance forced by the civil war. Although they destroyed part of the city's fortified complex and inflicted heavy casualties on the garrison, the town withstood the siege and the crusading army was forced to retreat to Königsberg in late October before winter set in. Two years later, when Vytautas and Jogaila were reconciled, the pact with the Order was broken and once again the brethren faced a united Samogitian and Lithuanian front.

The Order's troops besieged Vilnius again in 1394, but were driven back by Polish-Lithuanian forces and two years later another truce was signed with Vytautas, who in 1398 finally ceded Samogitia to the Order in exchange for the brethren's military aid against the Golden Horde. The recently deposed khan, Tokhtamysh, had sought Vytautas's help against his rival in exchange for accepting Lithuanian lordship over Ruthenia. Following initial military successes, Vytautas successfully petitioned the pope to frame his campaign as a crusade. Vytautas also renounced Lithuanian influence over Pskov in favour of the Livonian brethren, which ultimately pushed the Rus' city state under the influence of Muscovy. The Order's brethren joined Vytautas's army, but in August 1399 the crusader host was defeated and the Mongol army reached the walls of Kyiv. Abandoning his territorial ambitions in Ruthenia, Vytautas once again made peace with his cousin and acknowledged the Polish-Lithuanian union, having previously sought to maintain Lithuania's complete autonomy.

The 'Great War' (1409–11)

Not long after Vytautas had renewed his alliance with Jogaila, in March 1401 the Samogitians (with the Lithuanian duke's encouragement) rebelled against the Order, prompting another conflict until a peace was agreed in 1404, with the brethren retaining control of the territory. Then in May 1409 a second Samogitian uprising was supported by Lithuanian and Polish forces. Grand Master Ulrich of Jungingen had already anticipated conflict and in August declared war on Poland. This conflict came to be known as the 'Great War'. The Order's armies ravaged the Dobrin Land and northern Kuyavia, as well as Masovian territories. The following year Polish and Lithuanian forces, accompanied by a contingent of Mongols, attacked the Order's territory. On 15 July both sides met near the villages of Grünfelde (Pol. Grunwald) and Tannenberg (Pol. Stębark) in what became known as one of the most famous battles in European history: Grunwald for Poles, Tannenberg for Germans and Žalgiris for Lithuanians. The battle was a disaster for the Order. The grand master and several of the Order's leading officials were killed, with many others taken prisoner.

The Polish-Lithuanian force then headed to Marienburg, with a number of the Order's garrisons surrendering to them on the way. After two weeks they arrived to find the town of Marienburg had been deliberately destroyed by the Order to remove any shelter for the attackers. The Polish-Lithuanian army besieged the castle for two months, but the Order's garrison, led by the commander of Schwetz (Pol. Świecie), Henry of Plauen, put up an effective defence. On 19 September the siege was lifted and the forces of the union returned to Poland and Lithuania. The brethren then took back most of the castles that had been captured, but were defeated again by a Polish-Lithuanian army at the Battle of Koronowo on 10 October. Finally, in February 1411, both sides signed a peace treaty at Thorn, which ended the 'Great War'. The Order agreed to withdraw from Samogitia for as long as Vytautas and Jogaila lived, return the Dobrin Land to Poland, and pay a significant amount in compensation – a sum of 6 million Prague *groschen*. Trade would resume, along with efforts by the union to Christianize Lithuania and Samogitia. The Order's losses at Grunwald were memorialized in a chapel commissioned by Plauen, the new grand master, and dedicated to St Mary. Archaeologists and metal detectorists continue to find objects relating to the battle in the vicinity.[5]

The impact of Grunwald has been downplayed in recent scholarship, and indeed the failure to capture Marienburg ensured the Order held on to power. The agreement in Thorn was also a diplomatic success for the brethren, as they did not lose any of their core territory, even if Samogitia was out of their reach temporarily. However, the payments due to the Polish crown proved to stretch the Order's finances, prompting the grand master to raise taxes, which caused resentment from some of the leading

Peace treaty signed by Henry of Plauen, Władysław Jagiełło and Vytautas in Thorn, Prussia (Toruń, Poland), 1 February 1411.

cities in Prussia. The Order's own numbers were also heavily reduced as a result of the war and many of its supporters from among the urban elite had also been killed.[6] The Order would have to now have to rely more on mercenaries to garrison its castles, which proved to be increasingly expensive. The war also brought Vytautas and Jogalia closer together, and the Polish-Lithuanian union was consolidated further in 1413 with the Union of Horodło.

Further conflicts, 1414–35

Control over Samogitia remained in the foreground as both sides continued to demand territorial concessions, and Polish-Lithuanian armies raided the Order's Prussian lands, prompting another truce in October 1414. Attempts were made to resolve the conflict at the papal Council of Constance (1414–18) and a tentative peace endured until 1422. Polish-Lithuanian forces attacked the Order's Prussian lands in what was later called the 'Gollub War', reaching as far as Pomesania and Ermland.

A number of castles were captured, and after two months Grand Master Paul of Rusdorf sued for peace. A new treaty was agreed on 27 September on the shores of Lake Melno. Lithuanian authority over Samogitia was reaffirmed, fixing the eastern border of the Order's Prussian lands with the Lyck river as a major demarcation line.[7] Poland, which regained parts of Kuyavia, accepted the Order's possession of Pomerelia, the Kulmerland and the adjacent Michelauer Land.

There were several years of peace, but following the death of Vytautas in 1430, his successor Švitrigaila (Jogaila's brother) sought again to separate Lithuania from Poland. The Order continued its policy of seeking to destroy the union, and when Jogaila sent troops into Lithuania to confront Švitrigaila, the brethren supported the new duke. In August 1431 the Order's armies crossed the southern Prussian border and attacked Polish lands, burning the town of Inowrocław. When Jogaila and Švitrigaila agreed to a truce, the Order was left isolated, and suffered a further military defeat at Dąbki on 13 September. A short peace followed as diplomatic efforts resumed, and the Poles joined an alliance with the Hussites – a reform movement in Bohemia – the following year. Švitrigaila maintained his alliance with the Order, particularly its Livonian branch. Warfare broke out in 1433, with the Hussite army attacking the Order's lands in Pomerelia and the Neumark, seizing the town of Dirschau but failing to take Danzig (Pol. Gdańsk). Again, the Order sued for peace. When warfare broke out between Švitrigaila and Vytautas's brother Sigismund Kęstutaitis, the Order's Livonian brethren provided military support. Sigismund triumphed at the Battle of Vilkomir (also known as Ukmergé) on 1 September 1435. The Livonian master Franco Kerskorff and many of his officials were killed, and the Order was forced to the negotiating table in December with a treaty signed in Brześć Kujawski. The alliance with Švitrigaila was over, and the Order renounced any further attempts to interfere in

Lithuanian affairs. This defeat also spurred the various powers in Livonia to sign an agreement at Walk (Latv. Valka) to work more closely together in defence of the land. As part of the agreement, which was to last for six years, the Order ended its attempt to incorporate Riga's cathedral chapter into its ranks, and accepted a moratorium on the ongoing dispute regarding the ownership of Riga.

The Rise of the Towns

The leading towns of Prussia and Livonia had developed aspirations for autonomous rule at an early stage. Trade in these centres was dominated by a smaller number of powerful merchant families, who sat on town councils that provided a certain degree of autonomous government. This was even permitted in settlements organized under the Order's own Kulm Law. In Prussia, representatives of the leading towns and secular knights with holdings had already been summoned by the Order throughout the fourteenth century to discuss fiscal policy, but the six main towns that were also members of the Hanse – Kulm (Pol. Chełmno), Thorn (Pol. Toruń), Braunsberg (Pol. Braniewo), Elbing (Pol. Elbląg), Königsberg (Rus. Kaliningrad) and Danzig – also met regularly to discuss their internal trading interests as well as their representation in Hanseatic assemblies. These meetings resulted in the formulation of ordinances that had to be approved and implemented by the Order, whose members, especially the grand master, would occasionally attend and become involved in the business of the towns.

The knightly class of Prussia initially consisted of landowners with smallholdings and little income derived from them. They gradually constituted a cohesive group, but were rarely included in town assemblies before the fifteenth century. In 1397 a group of nobles in the Kulmerland formed the Lizard Union, a coalition aimed at opposing the Order's rule. Their efforts were unsuccessful and the leader of the Union, Nicholas of Renys, was executed by the Order in 1411. But the influence of both the towns and knights as collective social groups with political agency, which historians have called 'estates', grew significantly after the 'Great War'. The catalyst for this was the Order's changing financial situation and the need to impose taxes. In 1411 and 1412 Grand Master Henry of Plauen held assemblies of the Prussian towns and knights where demands for money were made in order to pay Poland. But having raised the money and paid it off eventually in three instalments, the Order went back to its mode of oligarchical rule, excluding its subjects from decision-making, especially regarding its foreign policy.

The principal change came in 1422 with the Treaty of Melno, which included a key clause that specified the knights and burghers of the Order's lands, including two Livonian towns – Reval (Est. Tallinn) and Goldingen (Latv. Kuldīga) – as well as those in Poland, would be the guarantors of peace. This was reaffirmed at Brześć Kujawski, where Polish and Prussian knights, clerics and town authorities swore an oath to uphold its terms, which they were to renew if the governing authority changed. In this way the 'estates' became guarantors of the peace between the Order and Poland-Lithuania. With their growing political agency, they also became more involved in the Order's foreign policy, exemplified by their participating in the sealing of treaties. By this time, knightly families in southern and western Prussia had become more actively involved in producing a surplus from their estates for sale, particularly grain, and so increasing their economic strength.[8]

The leading towns of Livonia had developed along similar trajectories to those in Prussia, particularly Riga, Dorpat (Est. Tartu) and Reval. Riga had been at odds with the Order's intent to dominate the town from an early stage, which saw the burghers destroy the brethren's castle on two occasions. The town's forces were defeated by the Order in both conflicts in 1330 and 1491. On both occasions the burghers were obliged to rebuild the Order's castle, although the master's residence would be relocated to Wenden (Latv. Cēsis). A manorial system had also begun to develop in Livonia, first on episcopal lands but eventually within the Order's commanderies, and by the fifteenth century the manors of the descendants of crusaders and German immigrants had become more numerous than those of native vassals.[9] John

Southern range of Cēsis castle, Latvia (Wenden, Livonia).

Ambundii, Archbishop of Riga from 1418 to 1424, was able to
bring the various representatives of the episcopates, landed vassals
and towns, as well as the Order, together for assemblies, but his
death saw the practice temporarily suspended. In 1495, when
the recently appointed Livonian master, Walter of Plettenberg,
and the Archbishop of Riga summoned the assembly in Walk,
which included representatives from Riga, Reval and Dorpat,
they focused on a common response to the defence of the land
against the threat of Muscovy. Plettenberg continued to lobby
the Livonian towns for support, and in the process of summoning
regular assemblies to discuss the matter, the *Landtag* gradually
became a regular forum for discussing Livonia's domestic and
foreign policies. This would eventually lead to a regulated assembly in the early decades of the sixteenth century.[10] However,
territorial divisions limited the development of a cohesive union
of Livonian towns and nobility, as the general assemblies became
places for negotiations between representatives from different
territories.[11] As a result, there was no possibility for a unified state,
which would eventually prove fatal during the Livonian War.

The Thirteen Years' War, 1454–66

In February 1440 representatives of the Prussian estates, the
nobility of the Kulmerland and the major Prussian towns, led by
Thorn and Kulm, met in Marienwerder and founded the Prussian
Confederation (Ger. *Preussischer Bund*), with the aim of publicly
challenging what was perceived as the Order's excessive fiscal
and political control. In secret, they also decided to switch their
allegiance to the Polish crown. The Confederation was declared
illegal by the imperial court in 1453, following petitioning from
Grand Master Ludwig of Erlichshausen, but it ignored the ver-
dict and did not disband. On 4 February 1454 the members of
the Confederation renounced their loyalty to the Order and
their armies attacked the Order's fortified convents in Thorn,

Ruins of the destroyed Teutonic Order's castle in Toruń, Poland
(Thorn, Prussia).

Graudenz (Pol. Grudziądz) and Elbing, whose garrisons quickly
surrendered. These castles were destroyed with gunpowder. This
was followed by uprisings in other towns, for example Rastenburg
(Pol. Kętrzyn), where the Order's procurator was seized by the
burghers and drowned.[12] The Confederation's envoys to the
Polish court in Cracow were warmly received, and on 6 March
King Casimir iv Jagiellon proclaimed Prussia's formal incorpo-
ration into Poland. This prompted the outbreak of the so-called
Thirteen Years' War. The Order benefited from German and
French financial support during this conflict, but ultimately a
string of defeats and a reliance on underpaid mercenaries resulted in the loss of Marienburg. The great castle was purchased
from its mercenary garrison by the city of Danzig, which then
handed it over to the Polish king, who rode in triumphantly on
8 June 1457. The town itself would be secured three years later.

   The grand master was forced to relocate his seat to Königsberg, far from the front line. The war, which dragged on until 1466,

saw numerous conflicts and short-lived truces. Some towns were attacked multiple times: for example Frauenburg (Pol. Frombork), where the Ermland chapter had declared its allegiance to the Polish king, was assaulted by the Order's force in 1454, taken back by Polish forces in 1455, then attacked again by the Order in 1456, 1461 and 1462. Not everyone supported the Confederation. In Danzig, the Dominican monastery became the meeting place for those opposed to the alliance with Poland, particularly merchants and artisans who had prospered under the Order's rule. Their plans to overthrow the town council by force and return Danzig to the Order were unsuccessful.[13]

Eventually, months of peace negotiations concluded with the Second Peace of Thorn on 19 October 1466. The treaty favoured Poland, which claimed Pomerelia and the Kulmerland, as well as large swathes of territory on the eastern bank of the Vistula, including Marienburg and Elbing. The Ermland bishopric and part of the Kulm episcopate were also subjugated to Poland. As a result, the Order lost more than half of its Prussian territories. The grand master was also obliged to take an oath of loyalty to every Polish monarch, and to provide military assistance to Poland when called upon. Thorn, which had been the Order's first urban colony, lost its leading position in the Prussian Hanseatic network and was forced to realign its trade with Kuyavia and Masovia.[14]

Internal Struggles in Livonia

The early decades of the fifteenth century were characterized by an internal struggle for the leadership of the Order's Livonian branch between two factions – Rhinelanders and Westphalians. The former group was made up of recruits from a number of regions, including the Dutch bailiwick of Utrecht. This, in turn, would have implications for the relationship between the Order's two Baltic branches. The Rhineland faction, which dominated

(*above*) Major territorial boundaries in medieval Livonia showing the Order's houses, and (*opposite*) numbers of brother-knights documented in 1451.

for the first three decades of the fifteenth century, was broadly pro-Prussian, while the Westphalians sought more autonomy for the Livonian brethren. Livonian forces had not been able to reach Prussia in time for the Battle of Grunwald, but were later involved in the retaking of the Order's castles from Polish-Lithuanian forces, and many brethren presumably remained to reinforce the garrisons. In 1433 an outbreak of plague in Livonia further reduced the number of brethren. At that point Master Cisse van den Rutenberg actively recruited in the Utrecht baili-wick, with the result that by 1435 a sixth of the Livonian brethren were Dutch.[15]

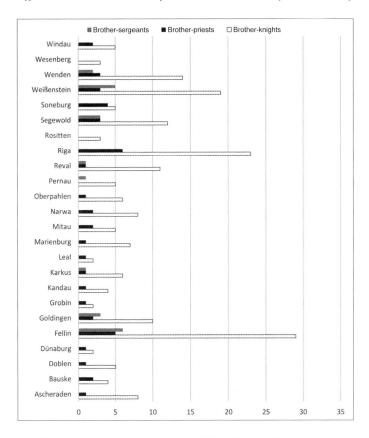

Over the next few years the Westphalian faction gained control over the Order's Livonian branch, and in 1438 succeeded in appointing a new master from their ranks. Those in the Rhineland faction still in positions of authority were gradually sidelined and removed from high offices, with the Westphalians coming to dominate the Order's Livonian branch by the mid-fifteenth century. By this time the Order was relying heavily on mercenaries to shore up its garrisons, and a visitation in 1451 indicated that only six Livonian convents – Fellin (Est. Viljandi), Goldingen, Riga, Segewold (Latv. Sigulda), Weißenstein (Est. Paide) and Wenden (Latv. Cēsis) – housed a dozen or more brother-knights.

The Order also continued its long-running conflict with the Archbishop of Riga. In 1448 Silvester Stodewescher, the former chaplain of the grand master, was appointed to Riga's see following the Order's lobbying and bribery at the papal court. The brethren sought to use him to bring the cathedral chapter under its influence again, but Stodewescher turned against the Order and the dispute over the control of the city continued. In 1452 the Order came to an agreement with the archbishop at Kirchholm (Latv. Salaspils) and subdivided the overlordship of Riga between them, which included various privileges and financial benefits, severely limiting the political autonomy of the burghers. The Order's commander of the Riga convent was also granted the right to participate in the town council. This has been interpreted as a response to the rise of the Prussian Confederation, with the aim of preventing a similar uprising in Livonia.[16] The Livonian towns did, however, offer to mediate in the conflict, while also offering some financial support to the Order. The Order agreed to postpone its conflict with Riga, and the brethren's Estonian vassals and the town of Reval acted as guarantors of the treaty. The Livonian master confirmed the settlement with Riga two years later.

However, both the Order and archbishop continued to seek more influence over Riga, while the city's patricians sought more autonomy. The dispute came to a head when the archbishop obtained military aid from Sweden. Following his defeat, he was imprisoned by the Order in 1479 and died soon after his release. Then, in October 1481, the burghers of Riga attacked the Order's castle and tried to block the brethren's trade through the town. War broke out and Riga's army defeated the Order's troops near Dünamünde (Latv. Daugavgrīva) on 22 March 1485. Further negotiations involved Hanseatic delegations, but eventually war would break out again and under Plettenberg's leadership, then as the Livonian marshal, Riga's forces would be defeated in 1491.

On 31 March an agreement was reached between Riga and the Order in Wolmar (Latv. Valmiera). With the exception of Riga, historian Juhan Kreem has suggested the reason other Livonian towns subordinated to the Order's rule, and did not rebel in the same way as the Prussian Confederation, was that their political and financial problems were not as severe. The balance of power in Livonia had also long depended on consensus, reiterated in the various agreements between the major powers in the fifteenth century.[17]

The fifteenth century also saw increasing political autonomy for the Livonian brethren. The grand master in Prussia steadily lost control over the appointment of the Livonian master, and after 1438 he was only able to confirm the candidate chosen by the Livonian chapter. The Livonian master had complete control over recruitment and appointments, but his governance required the assistance of the marshal and the commanders of the most important convents, limiting his role in policy making. Then, in 1459, the grand master nominally presented the Order's lands in north Estonia to the Livonian master, and absolved its vassals and towns from their oath to the grand master. The former Danish lands had been under the de facto control of the Order's Livonian branch for more than a century, but this symbolic gesture was an important concession from the grand master.

Gold coin of Walter of Plettenberg (master of the Livonian Order, 1494–1535), produced in Riga in 1535. It shows the Livonian master on one side and the Virgin Mary and Child on the other.

Nonetheless, the status of north Estonia remained unclear and the grand master still appears to have claimed overlordship over the region.[18] The struggle for more political autonomy from Prussia culminated in the reign of Walter of Plettenberg (1494–1535). In exchange for providing financial support to the brethren in Prussia, the Livonian branch of the Order demanded complete control over the elections of their master and the confirmation of their overlordship over the Order's Estonian lands. This would culminate in a charter, issued by the last Prussian grand master on 29 September 1520, which met the demands of the Livonian brethren. This would finally be confirmed in 1525, after which Plettenberg toured Estonia, receiving homage from his vassals.

The Beginning of the End

Conventual life came to an end in the western part of the Order's (now former) Prussian territories in 1466. Those castles that came under Polish control were converted into residences for royal officials. The largest continued in their role as administrative centres, although completely stripped of their earlier monastic character. Commanderies and other major districts were reorganized as elderships or *starostwa*. Western Prussia now became known as Royal Prussia and the Order was reduced to its eastern commanderies, with the grand master's seat now firmly established in Königsberg. In the last decades of the fifteenth century the Order concentrated its efforts on developing its eastern frontier, with the creation of new administrative districts and the encouragement of settlement. This resulted in increased competition over the control of the borderland districts and their inhabitants between the Order's officials and the lord lieutenant of Samogitia.[19] With the Order severely weakened, the estates increasingly exercised political power. A distinctive knightly class emerged in eastern Prussia, whose descendants would eventually come to be known as Junkers.[20]

By this time the Order's Livonian branch was essentially acting independently, as the Prussian brethren became heavily reliant on Poland and had lost their standing on the international stage. The reigns of the last two Prussian grand masters of the Order – Frederick of Saxony and Albert of Hohenzollern – saw attempts to break away from Polish influence and challenge the legitimacy of the Second Peace of Thorn, demanding the return of territories lost to Poland. In the early decades of the fifteenth century the brethren were still promoting themselves (and being perceived) as crusaders. The war against Poland-Lithuania in 1409–11 had been promoted as a crusade against pagans and schismatics, and the brethren defended their crusading role at the Council of Constance (1414–18), where the Polish-Lithuanian delegation argued for the Order to redirect its crusading efforts against Mongols and Turks. Yet by the end of the fifteenth century secularization of the Order's Prussian branch was, in many respects, inevitable.[21]

NINE

The Reformation and the End of the Teutonic Order's Rule in the Baltic

y the turn of the sixteenth century the Teutonic Order's Prussian branch was in decline, but it was also being irreversibly transformed by its leadership. The Peace of Thorn in 1466 had left the brethren with the least productive lands in their former territory, reducing their income and, in turn, the ability to support their own members. Recruitment had already been falling and this was exacerbated in the last decades of the fifteenth century. Many of those who governed over districts treated their offices as if they were their own private domains, increasing their personal income as they aspired to the quality of life enjoyed by their aristocratic counterparts in the empire. They also began to align their interests with the noble families of Prussia, many of whom were descended from the mercenaries brought in by the Order during the wars against Poland-Lithuania. The grand masters who reigned after 1466 sought to renew the Order's sense of purpose and to revive their brethren's spirituality, but to no avail. Before he died in 1497, Grand Master John of Tiefen urged the Order to seek his replacement from one of the great noble houses of the empire. He hoped this would provide for stronger leadership and, as vassals of the emperor, ensure the Order could strive for independence from Poland. Tiefen proposed Frederick, the younger son of Duke Albert of Saxony. Frederick was duly admitted to the Order in Ulm in May 1498, with the approval of both the emperor and the king of

Poland, John I Albert. His election to the office of grand master then took place in Königsberg at the end of September.[1]

Frederick arrived with his own entourage from Saxony, which included his chancellor Dietrich of Werthern. He sidelined the Order's other high officials and began to govern as if he were ruling over a secular princely court. In a symbolic gesture that foreshadowed the branch's secularization in the coming decades, Frederick replaced the image of the Virgin, the Order's divine patron and sovereign, with his own family arms. He also made his intentions towards Poland-Lithuania very clear, refusing to take the oath of vassalage to John. When the emperor declared the Peace of Thorn was invalid, John had had enough and sent an army to Thorn (Pol. Toruń), forcing the Order to the negotiating table, but died not long after in June 1501. His successor, Alexander Jagiellon, had already made an alliance with the Order's Livonian branch, but was distracted by a war with Muscovy and would reign for only four years. Grand Master Frederick died in 1510, but not before discussions had begun regarding his replacement with the Margrave of Brandenburg-Ansbach, who was keen on his third son Albert taking up the office. The emperor also favoured this choice for the new grand master, as did the Bishop of Pomesania, who headed the Order's regency.

On 13 February 1511 Albert was admitted into the Order and elected as the grand master in Königsberg on 6 July. Aged 21, he would be the youngest to hold the office. However, he was elected *in absentia* and would not arrive in Prussia for another year and a half. Like his predecessor, Albert continued to introduce secular features to the Order's governance, and his principal advisor was a Saxon nobleman, Dietrich of Schönberg. Albert also continued Frederick's policy of refusing to acknowledge Poland's overlordship and contesting the territorial divisions imposed on the Order's Prussian lands in 1466. In 1512, when Lithuania was invaded by Muscovite forces, Albert refused to send aid. Instead, he frantically set about gathering imperial support for his position, and even entered into an alliance with Muscovy; by 1515, however, Emperor Maximilian had reconciled himself with the Polish king Sigismund I the Old, who was trying to find support for his ongoing war with Muscovy, and even suggested that Albert offer his submission to Sigismund. Albert refused and Schönberg began to implement taxation and military levies in preparation for war with Poland. In 1519, when Albert demanded the return of the territories lost in 1466, the Polish *Sejm* (parliament) declared war on Prussia. The so-called *Reiterkrieg* (Knight's War) began when Albert's forces attacked Ermland at the end of December. In response, Sigismund's army entered Pomesania in what became a tit-for-tat conflict that dragged on for fourteen months. Albert, with the support of German princes, recruited a substantial army of mercenaries, but failed to take the strategically key towns of Heilsberg (Pol. Lidzbark Warmiński) and Danzig (Pol. Gdańsk). When Ottoman troops invaded Hungary, Emperor Charles V demanded Albert and Sigismund end their conflict and focus on the common enemy of Christendom. A truce was signed on 5 April 1521.

Reformation and the End of Theocratic Prussia

Following a temporary end to the hostilities, Albert travelled again to the empire in search of new allies against Poland-Lithuania, where he encountered some of the leading figures of the Reformation.[2] In 1522, in the free imperial city of Nuremberg, he heard a sermon from the Protestant reformer Andreas Osiander, then in 1523 and 1524 he travelled to Wittenberg where he met with Martin Luther, who eventually convinced him to secularize the Order's territories in Prussia and sever all ties with the Catholic Church. In March 1523 Luther had published an open letter to the lords of the Teutonic Order, calling on them to abandon celibacy as part of his broader attack on monastic life. He recommended two of his reformist colleagues to Albert: John Briessmann, a former Franciscan, and John Amandus, a priest and rhetorician. Both travelled to Königsberg and preached sermons there to eager congregations, although they fell out with each other and Amandus, who acquired a reputation for inciting riotous behaviour in his listeners, would eventually leave. Briessmann appears to have had a profound influence on the Bishop of Samland, George Polentz, who would go on to preach reformist ideas himself and encourage the burghers of Königsberg to read Luther's writings. When news of this reached the Holy See, the pope ordered Albert to reprimand Polentz, which he did in public while encouraging his reformist activities in private. Albert had already been convinced by Luther's arguments and with the help of Polentz, who began sending preachers to spread Lutheranism in other parts of Prussia, the Reformation took root in the leading cities of the Prussian *Ordensland*. In the summer of 1524, the Lutheran preacher George Speratus arrived in Königsberg and would later become the Protestant bishop of Pomerania. The following year religious paintings were removed from the cathedral and Old Town church in Königsberg, and liturgical vessels were taken from the churches into the care of the town's guilds. The Order's capital was fast becoming a Lutheran city.

In Cracow, the royal capital of Poland, Albert signed a peace treaty with Sigismund on 8 April 1525, swore allegiance to him and symbolically handed over his robe of office, finally ending the long-standing conflict between the two powers. The new duke renounced his oath of loyalty to the papacy and was shortly followed by most of the remaining Prussian brethren. Eastern Prussia was now under the secular governance of the Hohenzollerns and was a vassal state of the Polish Crown. Sigismund, however, had not demanded the transformation of the Order's territory into a secular, hereditary duchy as part of the deal. This was very much Albert's initiative, and the Polish king was fearful of Lutheranism spreading within his own realm, but realized there was nothing he could do to prevent its proliferation in Prussia. He did, however, try to warn Albert that his apostasy would result in significant political problems. His hope was, however, that it would be easier to bring back Catholicism to the Duchy of Prussia now that it was a Polish fief. The pope too did not protest against the secularization of Prussia, accepting Albert's submission, and instead appealed to Sigismund to reinstate Catholicism in the new duchy.[3]

From 26 to 31 May Albert gave an account of his submission to the Prussian *Landtag* assembled at Königsberg, now the capital of the duchy, where the estates also swore the oath of allegiance. Then, in an unprecedented (but not unexpected) move, the Bishop of Samland relinquished his own secular authority over his diocese to the duke, in keeping with Lutheran thought on the power of the state. The diocese of Pomesania would follow suit two years later. The Order's emblem of the black cross was replaced by a black eagle with a gold crown around its neck, bearing the letter 'S' (for Sigismund). The eagle, which had featured on the arms of the grand master, simultaneously expressed earlier links with the Holy Roman Empire and the redefined allegiance to the Polish crown. On 6 July Albert officially declared his support for Lutheranism and in December announced a statute that redefined the organization of the Prussian Church on his lands.[4] This document was informed by Briessmann, who would also come to play a leading role in the introduction of Lutheranism into Livonia.

Lutheranism spread quickly among the duchy's urban elites, but was slow to reach rural communities, especially in the eastern borderlands with Lithuania. As in other regions affected by the Reformation, the Catholic trappings of churches began to be stripped away, wall paintings were limewashed and religious sculptures were destroyed. Tiles decorated with the leading figures

Lucas Cranach the Elder, *Albert of Brandenburg-Ansbach (Hohenzollern),
Duke of Prussia*, 1528, oil on wood.

of the Reformation became popular on the urban market.[5] The
ducal court in Königsberg became a focus for patronage of the
arts and sciences, which included astrology and alchemy, and a
university would be established there in 1544. While the duchy
bordered with Catholic Polish and Lithuanian territories, there
is no evidence of religious hostilities between Lutherans and

Catholics, although eventually Jesuits would establish themselves here as part of the Counter-Reformation, encouraged by the rulers of Poland-Lithuania.[6]

The Order's system of territorial administration was replaced by the new administrative regions of Samland, Lower and Upper Prussia, which in turn were each subdivided into elderships, the system of governance used in Poland and one that had been introduced into Royal Prussia in 1466. There were also changes aimed at integrating the monetary systems of Poland, Royal Prussia and Ducal Prussia: from 9 June 1530 the Order's coinage was officially declared invalid.[7] Demographic changes in the Polish and Lithuanian borderlands, which had already begun in the late fifteenth century, accelerated following the cessation of hostilities. Peripheral urban centres such as Memel were able to flourish.[8] In eastern Prussia the exploitation of woodland resources began in earnest at this time, as the settlements mushroomed, with the clear demarcation of forest ownership along with rights for cutting timber and hunting, alongside evidence for poaching. Those who settled within the duchy maintained their allegiance to Albert.[9] The remnants of the Prussian population continued to maintain some form of identity in rural villages into the sixteenth and early seventeenth centuries. This is mentioned in contemporary accounts, most notably Simon of Grunau's *Preussische Chronik*, which describes the persistence of native religious practices, particularly in Samland.

The Order's fortified convents in eastern Prussia and the residences of procurators were repurposed for the governance of the new duchy, with the most important becoming residences for the new office of elder. In the process, many were remodelled or restored following damage sustained in earlier conflicts. For example, the Order's castle at Mohrungen (Pol. Morąg) became the residence of an elder in 1525. Under the direction of architect Blesius Bewart, two or three new wings were built with three tall corner towers, forming a spiral around the central courtyard, with the whole structure plastered over. Within, parts of the timber ceiling painted in polychrome, dating to the mid-sixteenth-century phase of restoration, were uncovered during modern conservation work. The castle would be abandoned at the start of the seventeenth century with the construction of a new palace in the town, and would slowly be dismantled. Further east, at Lötzen (Pol. Giżycko), the Order's procurator was also replaced by an elder. The castle had been destroyed in 1520 when it was abandoned by its garrison; renovations in 1560 included the addition of a new 'Renaissance' facade to the principal building, which would later be converted into a hunting lodge. Four small wings with residential and service functions were also added.[10] Life in these fortified residences completely changed, no longer defined by a fading monastic lifestyle.

Lutheranism in Livonia

At the start of the sixteenth century tensions between Livonia and Muscovy were at an all-time high following Ivan III's sacking of Novgorod and his closure of its Hanseatic kontor. Walter of Plettenberg, hailing from a Westphalian family, had risen up the ranks of the Order in Livonia, becoming master in 1494. He subsequently made an alliance with Alexander Jagiellon against Muscovy and appealed to the pope for a crusading indulgence to fund his military campaign, with the justification that the Russians were schismatics and therefore viable targets for a holy war. His appeal was supported by the Archbishop of Riga and the grand master, but no indulgence was immediately forthcoming. In the event, Plettenberg demonstrated his military skills on the battlefield, winning significant victories against the Russians at the Battle of Siritsa River in 1501 and then again at Smolin in 1502, which eventually led to a truce. The following year, Pope Alexander VI finally granted the requested indulgence for a period of three years, which his successor Julius II confirmed in 1504. The indulgence was to be offered in all towns around the Baltic Sea and all those belonging to the Hanse, as well as the dioceses of Riga, Magdeburg, Bremen, Kammin and Reval (Est. Tallinn). The amount raised was substantial enough that it encouraged Plettenberg to apply for a second indulgence in 1506. This was granted and preaching and collecting money continued until 1510. Recipients of the indulgence were expected to fight for six months at their own expense, to pay someone to do so on their behalf, or to pay a sum following an assessment by the preacher of the indulgence. But there was no more fighting, and the peace with Muscovy would hold for half a century. When the armies of Ivan IV (the Terrible) invaded Livonia in 1558, in what became known as the devastating Livonian War, the outcome for the Order would be profound and irreversible.

Before then, already during Plettenberg's reign, the Reformation was slowly taking root in Livonia, particularly in Riga and Courland, but eventually in the other major towns.[11] In 1521, the same year Pope Leo X condemned Luther's teachings, the first German Lutheran preachers arrived in Reval. In 1523 Luther's student Herman Marsow began preaching in Dorpat (Est. Tartu), and the following year a union between Estonian towns and some of the Order's vassals was established to support the growing Reformation, although Plettenberg disapproved of any public opposition to the Holy See. The Lutheran preacher Andreas Knöpken was elected as archdeacon of St Peter's church in Riga by the town council in 1524 and began to preach reformist ideas. Archbishop Jasper Linde was unable to prevent his appointment or subsequent activities.

Then in April 1525 events in Prussia shook the Order's remaining branches. In Livonia, Plettenberg made a bid for the grand master's position but, evidently lacking the ambition to rule, quickly conceded to the German master. That summer Duke Albert sent a delegation to Livonia led by Fredrick of Haydeck to explain his submission to the Polish king, and to encourage Plettenberg to do likewise.[12] The delegation did not move the Livonian master and upon his return Haydeck wrote *Christlich Ermahnung*, which was addressed to Plettenberg, praising him for allowing the Word of God to be preached, but admonishing him for not going further and also criticizing the Order's rules. Copies would eventually be sent to Livonia for widespread circulation, with the aim of promoting the Lutheran cause. Meanwhile, the secretary of Riga's town council, John Lohmüller, wrote to the Livonian marshal John Plater (although addressing the entire leadership of the branch, including the master), as well as the Bishop of Samland, setting out a blueprint for the Reformation of Livonia. At its core was the argument that religious authorities, particularly the pope and bishops, should not wield secular authority, and that the Order in Livonia should remain intact as a secular institution and exercise power as the sole ruler. It was an attractive argument for breaking the power of the Livonian bishops. Indeed, the Order's Livonian branch was increasingly viewed as a secular, knightly organization, rather than a monastic one.[13] At the same time there was a general fear in Livonia of the rule of princely dynasties, and resistance to the election of a princely figure to the Order's leadership from the Archbishop of Riga and the estates. The Livonian leadership was slowly edging in this direction. Plettenberg had been made an imperial prince and emphasized his personal rule increasingly through public ceremony, although he remained an elected figure within his aristocratic peer group, the first among equals. His successors came from the magnate families of Brandenburg and Mecklenburg.[14]

In 1527 Briessmann finally arrived in Riga and helped Knöpken push through reforming ideas. Several years later he would compile a liturgy for the leading Livonian towns – Riga,

Reval and Dorpat – based on those developed for the Lutheran Church in Prussia. In comparison, however, the spread of reforming ideas was much slower in Livonia. This was due to the fact there were fewer towns, as well as significant linguistic and social barriers between the smaller German and substantially larger native population. In the following century, much of the latter lived in the countryside and was regarded by Lutherans as clinging to Catholic and pagan 'superstitions'. Within the Order, interest in Lutheranism slowly grew. The commander of Windau (Latv. Ventspils), William of Balen, became the first high-ranking brother in Livonia to join the reformers, and several other members of the Order also abandoned Catholicism. Balen was eventually demoted and transferred to Talkhof (Est. Puurmani), but the presence of Lutherans within the Order was generally tolerated, as the main concern for the Westphalian faction, now dominating the leadership in Livonia, was one of autonomy from Prussia rather than of religious division. Instead, those who were pro-Prussian or with contacts to Duke Albert were singled out, as they were perceived to be a threat to the Order's independence in Livonia.

While Plettenberg was a committed Catholic, his successors were more receptive to Lutheran ideas and they encouraged preachers to come to Livonia. When the Master John of Recke died in 1551, both the emperor and the Order's grand master urged for the election of a true Catholic. But the next master, Henry of Galen, supported Lutheranism and took part in evangelical services in Riga. Reformist ideas were clearly not perceived as a threat to the Order's integrity in Livonia. This is perhaps the clearest evidence for its transformation into an aristocratic, chivalric organization, one which could accommodate different religious denominations.

The Livonian War and Secularization

In January 1558 the Muscovite invasion of north Livonia was the catalyst for the secularization of the Order's remaining Baltic branch. The Order was unable to effectively mobilize its military resources and in the face of a string of Russian victories, the brethren debated how best to deal with the threat. The marshal Jasper of Münster, pitched to succeed as master, argued for an alliance with Poland-Lithuania but was opposed and outmanoeuvred by a faction led by William of Furstenberg.[15] Another member of the pro-Polish-Lithuanian faction was Gotthard Kettler, who came from a lower noble family and had risen up the ranks of the Order to commander of Fellin (Est. Viljandi), becoming a member of the master's inner circle of advisors. Forcing the existing master to resign and taking his place, he had hoped for military aid from Poland-Lithuania against Muscovy. With north Estonia submitting to Sweden in 1561 (and eventually the whole of north Livonia in 1582), Kettler saw the only way to preserve his own authority was to make a formal alliance with Poland. In contrast to the previous masters, he was intent on preserving his own power, even at the expense of the Order. He had also secretly converted to Lutheranism.[16]

In 1561 Kettler entered into negotiations with the Polish king, who agreed to the establishment of the Duchy of Courland and Semigallia from the Order's lands south of the Daugava river. This region would come under royal overlordship in the same way as Ducal Prussia, with Kettler appointed as its first governor, while the rest would become incorporated into Poland-Lithuania. On 5 March 1562 Kettler handed over his personal insignia, seal and mantle to the representative of the Polish king in Riga, in a symbolic gesture of the dissolution of the Order's Livonian branch. This was followed by the new duke's property and control guarantees to the vassals of the former Order, and their declaration of

Reconstruction of the castle at Wenden, Livonia (Cēsis, Latvia),
c. 1550.

allegiance to the duke. With this act, 325 years of theocratic rule
in the eastern Baltic had come to an end. In order to establish
his hereditary line, Kettler married Anna, the daughter of the
Duke of Mecklenburg, and had a new residence built in Mitau
(Latv. Jelgava). He also appointed advisors such as Solomon
Henning, who contributed to the spread of reformist ideas in the
new duchy, protected under the agreement with the Polish king.
Kettler met with Philip Melanchthon, a leading figure of the
Lutheran Reformation, whose student Stephan Bülau became
the first preacher in the ducal court. He was responsible for the
first inspection of the new Protestant Church in Courland, which
resulted in a series of recommendations presented to the duke
in 1570. Kettler ordered the translation of confessional texts
into the Latvian language, which contributed to establishing its
status as a written language, and laid the foundations for Latvian
literature.[17]

The Teutonic Order in the Empire

At the time of the secularization of the Order's Prussian branch in 1525, the German province was led by Walter of Cronberg and consisted of a dozen bailiwicks located in the Rhineland, southern and central Germany, and Austria. With Albert's adoption of the ducal title, the office of grand master was claimed by both Cronberg and Walter of Plettenberg. Emperor Charles v intervened in the dispute and ultimately sided with Cronberg. The new grand master announced his claim over the Duchy of Prussia, which became a concern to the Polish king, especially when the emperor conferred on Cronberg the title of imperial prince and granted the Order's former lands to him as a fief. But these gestures proved to be futile, and Prussia remained lost to the Order. Cronberg also tried to recover the Order's holdings in Italy and Iberia, again with no success. In 1526 the Order's headquarters were relocated from Königsberg to the seat of the German master in Mergentheim, which itself had been relocated from Horneck the previous year.

The Order's German branch retained its former papal and imperial privileges, with added financial incentives. In the face of the challenges faced by the Reformation, the new grand master sought to reform the order and issued a new rule. A policy of religious tolerance was adopted and Protestant members were accepted into the brethren's ranks alongside Catholics, reflecting the connections between Catholics and Protestants within the great noble families of the empire. For the Order, quality of life and noble descent became far more important issues than religious differences.[18] The Order's grand masters remained Catholic nobles and the institution retained many of its estates as 'Catholic islands' within Protestant lands, and in this way retained a core Catholic identity. In other instances, there was fragmentation. A case in point is Utrecht, where even after the state joined the revolt against Spain and banned Catholicism, its nobility and urban elites continued to send their sons to the Teutonic Order, and as a result the bailiwick survived. New brother-priests were not permitted, and the public celebration of Mass was also forbidden. Eventually the bailiwick became fully Protestant and broke from the Order in the seventeenth century.[19]

The Teutonic Order remained a small but important institution, tied to the Habsburgs. Its grand masters continued to claim Prussia, and in the early seventeenth century Maximilian of Austria sought to revive the Order as a fighting force against the Turks. Mergentheim would remain the grand master's residence until 1809, when Napoleon dissolved the Teutonic Order within the territories of the Confederated States of the Rhine (*Rheinbund*). The grand master's seat was then relocated to Vienna, where the Order's principal Austrian house had been established in the early thirteenth century. It remains there to this day.

TEN

The Rise and Fall of a Medieval Religious Corporation

From its humble beginnings as a field hospital at the siege of Acre in 1190, the Teutonic Order grew and developed into one of the most powerful institutions in medieval Europe. Over the course of the thirteenth century, its forces were spread across multiple crusading frontiers, from the Mediterranean to the eastern Baltic. Against formidable odds the Order was able to establish itself as an independent ruler in the conquered tribal lands of northeastern Europe. Moreover, with the loss of the Holy Land in 1291, it was able to convincingly reinvent itself as the protector of Latin Christendom in northeastern Europe. This is exemplified by the regular stream of knights joining the seemingly endless war against pagans in Samogitia and Lithuania, a war that was envisaged as an ongoing crusade. Meanwhile in Marienburg, the Order built the largest castle in Christendom, representing the apogee of the brethren's power in the late fourteenth century and one of the most spectacular monuments of the Middle Ages, albeit one that has been heavily restored and modified since the late nineteenth century. Headed by the increasingly important figure of the grand master, the Order ruled as a collective, and, as the leading historian of the Teutonic Order, Udo Arnold, has written, governed its Baltic lands in the spirit of *Realpolitik* rather than as a missionary venture.[1]

In Prussia the Order developed into the strongest of the constellation of theocratic powers that governed the conquered territory. In Livonia, although the Order became the most powerful military force, it was never able to achieve the same level of political supremacy and had to share power with the episcopates, principal towns and the Danish king. In the empire, the Order did not wield any sovereign power, but was fully integrated into the Church. This is also the reason why scholarship has predominantly focused on the Order's Prussian branch, but it is important to remember that from its earliest decades the Order was a transnational organization. In Prussia the process of settlement in the countryside was dominated by peasants, and the Order prevented the establishment of a powerful class of landowning nobles. In Livonia, on the other hand, the peasantry was made up of the native population, and a noble class of vassals (both native and German) developed particularly on the lands of the episcopates, although most German speakers were confined to towns and castles. This resulted in a centralized government in Prussia versus a more decentralized group of powers who governed Livonia, each acting as a check on the power of the other, but also requiring consensus when it came to the defence of the land against external threats. The path to personal rule within the Order's Livonian branch took a similar form to that in Prussia, but the reorganization of the administration with an educated class of professional civil servants was much slower than in Prussia. The grand masters of the late fifteenth and early sixteenth centuries put the Order onto a path of secularization, one that became wedded to the Reformation taking hold in Prussia and Livonia. The Reformation was introduced in Prussia by Albert, but it did not take root in Livonia at this time, where the master held onto Catholicism.

The sixteenth century saw the secularization of the Teutonic Order's Prussian and Livonian branches, ending over three centuries of theocratic rule in the eastern Baltic. The Reformation played a key role in bringing the Order's existence in the eastern

Baltic to an end. The acceptance of Lutheranism by the two branches of the Order effectively ended the system of ecclesiastical organization within the newly created duchies that had defined the medieval *Ordensland*. Lutheran bishops continued to administer these dioceses into the later sixteenth century, and even with reorganization under Polish rule and the assertion of the Counter-Reformation, the resulting administration represented a break from the medieval episcopates. While the Order continued to function within the empire, its connection with the world of the *Milites Christi* was finally severed.

REFERENCES

1 The German Hospital of the Third Crusade

1 Thomas Asbridge, *The First Crusade: A New History* (London, 2012). For general histories of the crusades see Christopher Tyerman, *God's War: A New History of the Crusades* (London, 2007); Jonathan Phillips, *Holy Warriors: A Modern History of the Crusades* (New York, 2009); Thomas Asbridge, *The Crusades: The War for the Holy Land* (London, 2010).
2 Malcolm Barber, *The Crusader States* (New Haven, CT, 2012).
3 The Holy Roman Empire was the successor of East Frankia, the easternmost part of the Carolingian Empire, centred on what is today Germany. It consisted of a confederation of territories and states that expanded to include large swathes of Central Europe, under the nominal leadership of emperors. For a good introduction, see Joachim Whaley, *The Holy Roman Empire: A Very Short Introduction* (Oxford, 2018).
4 G. A. Loud, ed., *The Crusade of Frederick Barbarossa: The History of the Expedition of the Emperor Frederick and Related Texts* (London, 2010).
5 Andrew Jotischky, *Crusading and the Crusader States* (London, 2017), p. 168.
6 For the most comprehensive study of the Teutonic Order in the Levant, see Nicholas Morton, *The Teutonic Knights in the Holy Land, 1190–1291* (Woodbridge, 2009).
7 Anthony Luttrell, 'The Hospitaller Background of the Teutonic Order', *Ordines Militares*, 26 (2021), pp. 351–75 (p. 364).
8 Ibid.

2 Expansion and Loss in the Thirteenth Century

1 Helen Nicholson, 'The Role of Women in the Military Orders', *Militiae Christi: Handelingen van de Vereniging voor de Studie over de Tempeliers en de Hospitaalridders vzw*, 1 (2010), pp. 210–19.
2 Kristjan Toomaspoeg, 'Montfort Castle and the Order of the Teutonic Knights in the Latin East', in *Montfort: History, Early*

Research and Recent Studies of the Principal Fortress of the Teutonic Order in the Latin East, ed. Adrian Boas and Rabei Khamisy (Leiden, 2017), pp. 15–23 (p. 22).

3 Martin Wihoda, 'The Premyslid Dynasty and the Teutonic Order', in The Crusades and the Military Orders, ed. Zsolt Hunyadi and József Laszlovszky (Budapest, 2001), pp. 337–47 (p. 338).

4 Nicholas Morton, The Teutonic Knights in the Holy Land, 1190–1291 (Woodbridge, 2009), p. 49.

5 Kristian Molin, 'Teutonic Castles in Cilican Armenia: A Reappraisal', in The Military Orders, vol. III: History and Heritage, ed. Victor Mallia-Milanes (Aldershot, 2008), pp. 131–7.

6 Morton, The Teutonic Knights.

7 Indriķis Šterns, 'The Rule and Statutes of the Teutonic Knights', The Orb, https://the-orb.arlima.net, accessed 7 January 2023.

8 Rabei Khamisy, 'Archaeological Remains of the 1202 Earthquake in the Frankish Village of Tarphile/Khirbat al-Manḥata', Levant, XLIX/3 (2017), pp. 333–41.

9 Denys Pringle, Andrew Petersen, M. Dow and C. Singer, 'Qal'at Jiddin: A Castle of the Crusader and Ottoman Periods in Galilee', Levant, 26 (1994), pp. 135–66.

10 Adrian Boas, Archaeology of the Military Orders: A Survey of the Urban Centres, Rural Settlements and Castles of the Military Orders in the Latin East (c. 1120–1291) (London, 2006), pp. 61–3; Adrian Boas and Georg Melloni, 'New Evidence for Identifying the Site of the Teutonic Compound in Acre', in Acre and Its Falls: Studies in the History of a Crusader City, ed. John France (Leiden, 2018), pp. 69–89.

11 Morton, The Teutonic Knights, p. 18.

12 For the most comprehensive study of Montfort, see Boas and Khamisy, eds, Montfort.

13 Nicholson, 'The Role of Women', p. 212; Myra Miranda Bom, Women in the Military Orders of the Crusades (New York, 2012), pp. 32–5.

14 Morton, The Teutonic Knights, p. 18.

15 Klaus Militzer, 'The Role of Hospitals in the Teutonic Order', in The Military Orders, vol. II: Welfare and Warfare, ed. Helen Nicholson (London, 1998), pp. 51–9 (p. 54).

3 A New Frontier

1 Harald Zimmermann, *Der Deutsche Orden im Burzenland: Eine diplomatische Untersuchung* (Cologne, 2000); Zsolt Hunyadi, 'The Teutonic Order in Burzenland (1211–1225): New Re-Considerations', in *L'Ordine Teutonico tra Mediterraneo e Baltico: Incontri e scontri tra religioni, popoli e culture*, ed. Hubert Houben and Kristjan Toomaspoeg (Galatina, 2008), pp. 151–62 (pp. 152–3).

2 Franz Zimmermann and Carl Werner, eds, *Urkundenbuch zur Geschichte der Deutschen in Siebenbürgen*, vol. 1 (Hermannstadt, 1892), p. 11.

3 Ioan Marian Ţiplic, 'Cavalerii teutoni şi fortificaţiile lor din Ţara Bârsei', *Corviniana*, 6 (2000), pp. 138–59; József Laszlovszky and Zóltan Soós, 'Historical Monuments of the Teutonic Order in Transylvania', in *The Crusades and the Military Orders*, ed. Zsolt Hunyadi and József Laszlovszky (Budapest, 2001), pp. 319–36; Adrian Ionita, *Feldioara-Marienburg: contributii arheologice la istoria Ţării Bârsei* (Bucharest, 2004).

4 Hunyadi, 'The Teutonic Order in Burzenland', pp. 161–2.

5 László Pósán, 'Prussian Missions and the Invitation of the Teutonic Order into Kulmerland', in *The North-Eastern Frontiers of Medieval Europe*, ed. Alan V. Murray (London, 2016), pp. 429–48 (pp. 439–41).

6 Sylvain Gouguenheim, *Krzyżacy* (Malbork, 2012), pp. 120–24.

4 Holy War and Conquest

1 Iben Fonnesberg-Schmidt, *The Popes and the Baltic Crusades, 1147–1254* (Leiden, 2007).

2 Anu Mänd, 'Saints' Cults in Medieval Livonia', in *The Clash of Cultures on the Medieval Baltic Frontier*, ed. Alan V. Murray (Farnham, 2009), pp. 191–223 (p. 195).

3 Fonnesberg-Schmidt, *The Popes and the Baltic Crusades*, p. 138.

4 The two principal histories of the Baltic crusades in English are Eric Christiansen, *The Northern Crusades* (London, 1997), and William Urban, *The Teutonic Knights: A Military History* (London, 2003). See also Eva Eihmane, 'The Baltic Crusades: A Clash of Two Identities', in *The Clash of Cultures on the Medieval Baltic Frontier*, ed. Murray, pp. 37–52.

5 Marian Biskup, 'Etniczno-demograficzne przemiany Prus Krzyżackich w rozwoju osadnictwa w średniowieczu', in *Opera Minora: Studia z dziejów zakonu Krzyżackiego* (Toruń, 2002), pp. 129–50.

6 Andrzej Radzimiński, *Chrystianizacja i ewangelizacja Prusów: Historia i źródła* (Toruń, 2011).

7 Sławomir Wyszomirski and Jarosław Wenta, trans., *Piotr z Dusburga, Kronika ziemi pruskiej* (Toruń, 2011); Mary Fischer, trans., *The Chronicle of Prussia by Nicolaus von Jeroschin: A History of the Teutonic Knights in Prussia, 1190–1331* (Farnham, 2010); Jerry Smith and William Urban, trans., *The Livonian Rhymed Chronicle* (London, 2017); James Brundage, trans., *The Chronicle of Henry of Livonia* (New York, 2003).

8 Aleksander Pluskowski and Heiki Valk, 'The Archaeology of the Crusades in the Eastern Baltic', in *The Crusader World*, ed. Adrian Boas (London, 2015), pp. 568–92; Valter Lang and Heiki Valk, 'An Archaeological Reading of the Chronicle of Henry of Livonia: Traces, Contexts and Interpretations', in *Crusading and Chronicle Writing on the Medieval Baltic Frontier: A Companion to the Chronicle of Henry of Livonia*, ed. Marek Tamm, Linda Kaljundi and Carsten Selch Jensen (Farnham, 2011), pp. 291–316; Aleksander Pluskowski, *The Archaeology of the Prussian Crusade: Holy War and Colonisation*, 2nd edn (London, 2022).

9 Sylvain Gouguenheim, *Krzyżacy* (Malbork, 2012), pp. 129–31.

10 Fonnesberg-Schmidt, *The Popes and the Baltic Crusades*, p. 199.

11 Sven Ekdahl, 'Horses and Crossbows: Two Important Warfare Advantages of the Teutonic Order in Prussia', in *The Military Orders*, vol. II: *Welfare and Warfare*, ed. Helen Nicholson (Farnham, 1998), pp. 119–51.

12 Wojciech Chudziak and Jacek Bojarski, 'Chełmno i Toruń: Początki miast na ziemi chełmińskiej', *Archaeologia Historica Polona*, XXIII/83 (2015), pp. 83–105 (pp. 90–99).

13 Wojeciech Chudziak, *Wczesnośredniowieczna przestrzeń sakralna in Culmine na Pomorzu Nadwiślańskim* (Toruń, 2003), p. 179.

14 Marcin Wiewióra, 'Najstarsze fazy osadnictwa krzyżackiego na zamkach w Unisławiu, Zamku Bierzgłowskim i Starogrodzie: Studia nad osadnictwem obronnym na ziemi chełmińskiej w XIII wieku', *Archaeologia Historica Polona*, 26 (2018), pp. 239–64 (pp. 247–50).

15 Zbyszek Sawicki et al., 'Survival at the Frontier of Holy War: Political Expansion, Crusading, Environmental Exploitation and the Medieval Colonising Settlement at Biała Góra, North Poland', *European Journal of Archaeology*, XVIII/2 (2015), pp. 282–311.

16 Daniel Gazda, *Wielokulturowy obiekt warowny na Górze Zamkowej oraz gród cyplowy w Starym Dzierzgoniu: studia i materiały* (Warsaw, 2018).

17 Axel Ehlers, 'The Crusade against Lithuania Reconsidered',
in *Crusade and Conversion on the Baltic Frontier, 1150–1500*,
ed. Alan V. Murray (Farnham, 2001) pp. 21–44 (p. 29).

18 Grzegorz Białuński, *Studia z dziejów plemion pruskich i jaćwieskich*
(Olsztyn, 1999), p. 119.

19 Juhan Kreem, 'The Teutonic Order as a Secular Ruler in Livonia:
The Privileges and Oath of Reval', in *Crusade and Conversion
on the Baltic Frontier*, ed. Murray, pp. 215–32 (pp. 217–18).

20 Arvi Haak, 'Archaeological Data about the Viljandi Castle
in the Medieval and Early Modern Period', in *Viljandi ordulinnus
ja Lossimäed läbi aegade (The Teutonic Order's Castle and Castle Hills
in Viljandi through Time)*, ed. Viljandi Museum (Viljandi, 2015),
pp. 27–64 (Estonian and English).

21 Kaur Alttoa, 'On the Architecture of Viljandi Castle', in
Viljandi ordulinnus ja Lossimäed läbi aegade, ed. Viljandi Museum,
pp. 87–110.

22 Heiki Valk et al., 'Thirteenth Century Cultural Deposits at the
Castle of the Teutonic Order in Karksi', *Arheoloogilised välitööd
Eestis/ Archaeological Field Work in Estonia 2012* (Tallinn, 2013),
pp. 73–92 (Estonian and English).

23 Romas Jarockis, 'Semigallia, 1100–1400: A Review of
Archaeological and Historical Sources', in *Culture Clash or
Compromise? The Europeanisation of the Baltic Sea Area, 1100–1400
AD*, ed. Nils Blomkvist (Visby, 1998), pp. 45–53 (p. 52); Andris Šnē,
'The Medieval Peasantry: On the Social and Religious Position of
the Rural Natives in Southern Livonia (13th–15th Centuries)',
Ajalooline Ajakiri, 1/2 (2008), pp. 89–100 (pp. 91–2).

24 Muntis Auns, 'Acquisition of the Acquired: The Establishing of a
Real Administration in Livonia', in *Culture Clash or Compromise?*,
ed. Blomkvist, pp. 259–67 (p. 265).

5 Territorial Lords

1 Klaus Militzer, *Die Entstehung der Deutschordensballeien im Deutschen
Reich* (Marburg, 1981); Jürgen Sarnowsky, *Der Deutsche Orden*
(Munich, 2007), p. 57.

2 Heinrich von Treitschke, 'Das deutsche Ordensland Preußen',
Preußische Jahrbücher, 10 (1862), pp. 95–151; Reinhard Wenskus,
'Das Ordensland Preußen als Territorialstaat des 14. Jahrhunderts',
in *Der deutsche Territorialstaat im 14. Jahrhundert*, ed. Hans Patze,
vol. 1 (Frankfurt am Main, 1970), pp. 347–82.

3 Anu Mänd, 'Saints' Cults in Medieval Livonia', in *The Clash of Cultures on the Medieval Baltic Frontier*, ed. Alan V. Murray (Farnham, 2009), pp. 191–223 (p. 195).

4 Marian Dygo, 'The Political Role of the Cult of the Virgin Mary in Teutonic Prussia in the Fourteenth and Fifteenth Centuries', *Journal of Medieval History*, xv/1 (1989), pp. 63–80; Sławomir Joźwiak and Janusz Trupinda, *Organizacja żeycia na zamku krzyżeackim w Malborku w czasach wielkich mistrzóźw (1309–1457)* (Malbork, 2007), p. 273; Paweł Gancarczyk, 'Kultura muzyczna zakonu krzyżackiego w Prusach', in *Fundacje artystyczne na terenie Państwa Krzyżackiego w Prusach*, ed. Barbara Pospieszna (Pelplin, 2010), pp. 269–82.

5 Janusz Tandecki, 'Rozwój terytorialny państwa zakonnego w Prusach', in *Państwo zakonu krzyżackiego w Prusach: Władza i społeczeństwo*, ed. Marian Biskup et al. (Warsaw, 2009), pp. 105–9 (p. 106).

6 Joźwiak and Trupinda, *Organizacja żeycia*.

7 Sarnowsky, *Der Deutsche Orden*, p. 57.

8 Roman Czaja and Andrzej Radzimiński, eds, *Zakon krzyżacki w Prusach i Inflantach: podziały administracyjne i kościelne w xiii–xvi wieku* (Toruń, 2013); Eng. trans. as *The Teutonic Order in Prussia and Livonia: The Political and Ecclesiastical Structures, 13th–16th Century* (Toruń, 2015).

9 Marian Dygo, 'Początki i budowa władztwa zakonu krzyżackiego (1226–1309)', in *Państwo zakonu krzyżackiego w Prusach*, ed. Biskup et al., pp. 53–78 (p. 73).

10 Ibid., p. 74.

11 Sławomir Joźwiak, *Centralne i terytorialne organy władzy zakonu krzyżackiego w Prusach w latach 1228–1410: rozwój, przekształcenia, kompetencje* (Toruń, 2001); Sławomir Joźwiak and Janusz Trupinda, *Krzyżackie zamki komturskie w Prusach* (Toruń, 2012), p. 33.

12 Dygo, 'Początki i budowa', p. 59.

13 Joźwiak and Trupinda, *Krzyżackie zamki*, pp. 96–8.

14 Juhan Kreem, 'Mobility of the Livonian Teutonic Knights', in *Making Livonia: Actors and Networks in the Medieval and Early Modern Baltic Sea Region*, ed. Anu Mänd and Marek Tamm (London, 2020), pp. 158–69.

15 Janusz Tandecki, 'Zakon krzyżacki', in *Państwo zakonu krzyżackiego w Prusach*, ed. Biskup et al., pp. 405–19 (pp. 406–11).

16 Joźwiak, *Centralne i terytorialne organy*; Sławomir Joźwiak, 'Podziały administracyjne', in *Państwo zakonu krzyżackiego w Prusach*, ed. Biskup et al., pp. 132–7 (p. 137).

17 Dariusz Poliński, 'Castrum Starkenberg w świetle najnowszych
   badań nad krzyżackimi obiektami obronnymi', in *Życie
   społeczno-kulturalne w państwie Zakonu Krzyżackiego (XIII–XVI w.)*,
   ed. Jan Gancewski et al. (Olsztyn, 2016), pp. 7–24.

18 Sven Ekdahl, 'The Strategic Organization of the Commanderies
   of the Teutonic Order in Prussia and Livonia', in *La Commanderie:
   Institution des ordres militaires dans l'Occident médiéval*, ed. Anthony
   Luttrell and L. Pressouyre (Paris, 2002), pp. 219–42 (p. 228).

19 Jóźwiak and Trupinda, *Organizacja żeycia*, p. 25.

20 Grzegorz Białuński, *Osadnictwo regionu Wielkich Jezior Mazurskich
   od XIV do początku XVIII wieku – starostwo leckie (giżyckie) i ryńskie*
   (Olsztyn, 1996), p. 14.

21 Kristjan Toomaspoeg, 'Communication Between Centre and
   Periphery: The Example of the Italian Branch of the Teutonic
   Order (13th–16th Centuries)', *Ordines Militares*, XXV (2020),
   pp. 109–36.

22 Udo Arnold, 'Eight Hundred Years of the Teutonic Order', in
   The Military Orders, vol. I: *Fighting for the Faith and Caring for the
   Sick*, ed. Malcolm Barber (Aldershot, 1994), pp. 223–35.

23 Walther Ziesemer, ed., *Das gross Ämterbuch des deutschen Ordens:
   Mit Unterstützung des Vereins für die Herstellung und Ausschmückung
   der Marienburg* (Wiesbaden, 1968; repr. 2009).

24 Juhan Kreem, *The Town and Its Lord: Reval and the Teutonic Order
   (in the Fifteenth Century)* (Tallinn, 2002).

25 Eva Eihmane, 'Livonia and the Holy See in 13th–Early 15th
   Centuries: Centre and Periphery of Christendom', in *The Image of
   the Baltic: A Festschrift for Nils Blomkvist*, ed. Michael Scholz, Robert
   Bohn and Carina Johansson (Visby, 2012), pp. 23–40.

26 Wiesław Długokęcki, 'Społeczeństwo wiejskie', in *Państwo zakonu
   krzyżackiego w Prusach*, ed. Biskup et al., pp. 460–94.

27 Aleksander Pluskowski et al., 'Re-Organising the Livonian
   Landscape', in *Environment, Colonization, and the Baltic Crusader
   States*, ed. Aleksander Pluskowski (Leiden, 2019), pp. 207–29.

28 Hermann Aubin, 'The Lands East of the Elbe and German
   Colonization Eastwards', in *The Cambridge Economic History of
   Europe from the Decline of the Roman Empire*, vol. I: *Agrarian Life of
   the Middle Ages*, ed. Michael M. Postan (Cambridge, 1966),
   pp. 449–86 (p. 463).

29 Roman Czaja, 'Miasta inflanckie XVIII–XVI w', in *Zakon krzyżacki
   w Prusach i Inflantach*, ed. Czaja and Radzimiński, pp. 215–40
   (p. 220).

30 Andris Šnē, 'The Medieval Peasantry: On the Social and Religious Position of the Rural Natives in Southern Livonia (13th–15th Centuries)', *Ajalooline Ajakiri*, 1/2 (2008), pp. 89–100 (pp. 90–92); Andris Šnē, 'The Early Town in Late Prehistoric Latvia', in *The Reception of Medieval Europe in the Baltic Sea Region*, ed. Jörn Staecker (Visby, 2009), pp. 127–36 (p. 133).

31 Wiesław Długokęcki, 'Kolonizacja ziemi chełmińskiej, Prus i Pomorza Gdańskiego do 1410 r.', in *Państwo zakonu krzyżackiego w Prusach*, ed. Biskup et al., pp. 200–217 (p. 204).

32 Roman Czaja, 'Urbanizacja kraju', in *Państwo zakonu krzyżackiego w Prusach*, ed. Biskup et al., pp. 177–230.

33 Długokęcki, 'Społeczeństwo wiejskie', p. 462.

34 Roman Czaja, 'Rozwój osadnictwa miejskiego', in *Państwo zakonu krzyżackiego w Prusach*, ed. Biskup et al., pp. 370–83.

35 Joachim Stephan, 'Prusowie w gospodarstwie krzyżaków', in *Gospodarka ludów morza bałtyckiego starożytność i średniowiecze: Mare Integrans – Studia nad dziejami wybrzeży Morza Bałtyckiego*, ed. Michał Bogacki, Maciej Franz and Zbigniew Pilarczyk (Toruń, 2009), pp. 317–25.

36 Marian Biskup, 'Etniczno-demograficzne przemiany Prus Krzyżackich w rozwoju osadnictwa w średniowieczu', in *Opera Minora: Studia z dziejów zakonu Krzyżackiego* (Toruń, 2002), pp. 129–50 (p. 136).

37 Grzegorz Białuński, *Przemiany społeczno-ludnościowe południowo-wschodnich obszarów Prus Krzyżackich i Książęcych (do 1568 roku)* (Olsztyn, 2001), p. 50.

38 Marian Biskup, 'Bemerkungen zum Siedlungsproblem und den Pfarrbezirken in Ordenspreussen im 14–15 Jahrhundert', in *Die Rolle der Ritterorden in der Christianisierung und Kolonisierung des Ostseegebietes*, ed. Zenon Nowak (Toruń, 1983), pp. 35–56.

39 Antoni Czacharowski, 'Toruń średniowieczny (do roku 1454)', in *Toruń dawny i dzisiejszy: Zarys dziejów*, ed. Marian Biskup (Warsaw, 1983), pp. 31–131 (p. 72).

40 Heldur Palli, *Eesti rahvastiku ajalugu aastani 1712* (Tallinn, 1996), pp. 23 and 40; Indriķis Šterns, *Latvijas vēsture, 1290–1500* (Riga, 1997).

41 Roman Czaja and Zenon Nowak, 'Państwo zakonu krzyżackiego w prusach – próba charakterystyki', in *Zakon krzyżacki w Prusach i Inflantach*, ed. Czaja and Radzimiński, pp. 1–27 (p. 21).

42 Tandecki, 'Struktury i podziały', p. 177.

43 Kreem, *The Town and Its Lord*, pp. 21, 100.

44 Hellmann Manfred, 'Der Deutsche Orden und die Stadt Riga',
   in *Stadt und Orden. Das Verhältnis des Deutschen Ordens zu den
   Städten Livland, Preußen und im Deutschen Reich*, ed. Udo Arnold
   (Marburg, 1993), pp. 1–33.
45 Kreem, *The Town and Its Lord*, pp. 101–3.
46 Šnē, 'The Medieval Peasantry', pp. 94–5.
47 Czaja and Nowak, 'Państwo zakonu krzyżackiego', p. 20.
48 Sven Ekdahl, 'Horses and Crossbows: Two Important Warfare
   Advantages of the Teutonic Order in Prussia', in *The Military
   Orders*, vol. II: *Welfare and Warfare*, ed. Helen Nicholson (Aldershot,
   1998), pp. 119–51; Aleks Pluskowski et al., 'Late-Medieval Horse
   Remains at Cēsis Castle, Latvia, and the Teutonic Order's Equestrian
   Resources in Livonia', *Medieval Archaeology*, LXII/2 (2018),
   pp. 351–79.
49 Kreem, *The Town and Its Lord*, p. 104.

6 Power and Faith

1 Andris Caune and Ieva Ose, *Latvijas 12. gadsimta beigu – 17.
   gadsimta vācu piļu leksikons* (Riga, 2004); Ieva Ose, 'Research
   on Medieval Castles in Latvia: Achievements and Problems',
   Kunstiteaduslikke Uurimusi, 25 (2016), pp. 23–42; Marian Arszyński,
   'Zamki i umocnienia zakonu krzyżackiego i biskupów w inflantach',
   in *Zakon krzyżacki w Prusach i Inflantach: podziały administracyjne
   i kościelne w XIII–XVI wieku*, ed. Roman Czaja and Andrzej
   Radzimiński (Toruń, 2013), pp. 183–213; Christofer Herrmann,
   *Mittelalterliche Architektur in Preussenland: Untersuchungen zur Frage
   der Kunstlandschaft und -geographie* (Petersberg, 2007), p. 81; Bogusz
   Wasik, 'Budownictwo i architektura zamków krzyżackich w Prusach',
   in *Sapientia aedificavit sibi domum*, ed. Janusz Trupinda (Malbork,
   2019), pp. 364–83.
2 Christofer Herrmann, 'Kloster und Burg – die Architektur des
   Deutschen Ordens in Preußen und Livland', in *Glaube, Macht und
   Pracht: Geistliche Gemeinschaften des Ostseeraums im Zeitalter der
   Backsteingotik*, ed. Oliver Auge, Felix Biermann and Christofer
   Herrmann (Rahden, 2009), pp. 209–20 (p. 212).
3 For example, Dariusz Poliński, *Pień: Siedziba krzyżackich prokuratorów
   w ziemi chełmińskiej* (Toruń, 2013).
4 For summaries, see Marian Arszyński, *Budownictwo warowne zakonu
   krzyżackiego w Prusach (1230–1454)* (Toruń, 1995); Tomas Torbus,
   Die Konventsburgen im Deutschordensland Preussen (Munich, 1998).

5 Sławomir Jóźwiak and Janusz Trupinda, *Krzyżackie zamki komturskie w Prusach* (Toruń, 2012).

6 Marian Arszyński, 'Architektura warowna Zakonu Krzyżackiego w Prusach', in *Fundacje artystyczne na terenie państwa krzyżackiego w prusach*, ed. Barbara Pospieszna (Pelplin, 2010), pp. 7–45 (p. 44).

7 Herrmann, 'Kloster und Burg', p. 213.

8 Jerzy Frycz, 'Architektura zamków krzyżackich', in *Sztuka pobrzeża Bałtyku*, ed. Hanna Fruba (Warsaw, 1978), pp. 19–43 (p. 35).

9 Bernard Jesionowski, 'Dzieje budowlane skrzydła zachodniego w świetle obserwacji architektonicznych', in *Wileki refektarz na zamku średnim w Malborku: dzieje – wstrój – konserwacja*, ed. Janusz Trupinda (Malbork, 2010), pp. 13–30 (p. 17).

10 Alicja Chruścińska, Bernard Jesionowski, Hubert Oczkowski and Krzysztof Przegiętka, 'Using the TL Single-Aliquot Regenerative-Dose Protocol for the Verification of the Chronology of the Teutonic Order Castle in Malbork', *Geochronometria*, xxx/1 (2008), pp. 61–7.

11 Jan Gancewski, *Rola zamków krzyzackich w ziemi chelminskiej od polowy xiv wieku do 1454 roku* (Olsztyn, 2001), p. 88.

12 Kazimierz Pospieszny, 'Über den Gebrauch der Gebrannten erde zur Bildnerei: Warsztaty ceglarski i plastyka architektoniczna zamku w Malborku w xiii i xiv w', in *Cegła w architekturze środkowo-wschodniej Europy*, ed. Marian Arszyński and Mariusz Mierzwiński (Malbork, 2002), pp. 163–79.

13 Marcin Wiewióra, 'Długi wiek xiii – początki krzyżackiej murowanej architektury obronnej na ziemi chełmińskiej w świetle najnowszych badan', *Archaeologia Historica Polona*, 22 (2014), pp. 113–44; Marcin Wiewióra, 'Gród i zamek w państwie krzyżackim – miejsce tradycji czy tradycja miejsca?', *Archaeologia Historica Polona*, 24 (2016), pp. 195–231.

14 Kaur Alttoa, 'On the Architecture of Viljandi Castle', in *Viljandi ordulinnus ja Lossimäed läbi aegade (The Teutonic Order's Castle and Castle Hills in Viljandi through Time)*, ed. Viljandi Museum (Viljandi, 2015), pp. 87–110 (Estonian and English).

15 Herrmann, *Mittelalterliche Architektur*, pp. 81–3.

16 Arszyński, 'Architektura warowna', p. 42.

17 Gregory Leighton, *Ideology and Holy Landscape in the Baltic Crusades* (Leeds, 2022), pp. 101–59 and appendix; see also Waldemar Rozynkowski, *Omnes Sancti et Sanctae Dei: Studium nad kultem świętych w diecezjach pruskich państwa zakonu krzyżackiego* (Malbork, 2006).

18 Jóźwiak and Trupinda, *Krzyżackie zamki*, p. 48; Sławomir Jóźwiak
   and Janusz Trupinda, 'Czy rzeczywiście wbrew "tradycji"? O
   współczesnych badaniach nad zamkami krzyżackimi na tle ustaleń
   historiografii z XIX i I. połowy XX wieku', *Archaeologia Historica
   Polona*, 26 (2018), pp. 25–39 (p. 28).

19 Andres Tvauri, 'Late Medieval Hypocausts with Heat Storage
   in Estonia', *Baltic Journal of Art History*, 1 (2009), pp. 49–78
   (pp. 55–8).

20 Rafał Kochański, 'Fosy i mosty jako element obronności zamków
   krzyżackich w Prusach', *Materiały Zachodniopomorskie*, 46 (2001),
   pp. 457–81 (p. 473); Bogusz Wasik, 'Parchamy z zamków Krzyżackich-
   technika budowy i zabudowa', *Komunikaty Mazursko-Warmińskie*,
   II/288 (2015), pp. 269–80.

21 Kochański, 'Fosy i mosty', p. 473; Wasik, 'Parchamy z zamków'.

22 Gancewski, *Rola zamków*, p. 51.

23 Jóźwiak and Trupinda, *Krzyżackie zamki komturskie*, p. 202.

24 Sławomir Jóźwiak, 'Organizacja życia na zamku krzyżackim
   w późnym średniowieczu na przykładzie stołecznej warowni
   malborskiej', in *Sapientia aedificavit sibi domum*, ed. Janusz Trupinda
   (Malbork, 2019), pp. 288–310 (p. 295).

25 Wiesława Rynkiewicz-Domino, '1.2.8. Segment fryzu z dekoracją
   maswerkową. ok. 1320', in *Fundacje artystyczne na terenie Państwa
   Krzyżackiego w Prusach*, ed. Pospieszna, p. 30.

26 Ieva Ose, 'Die Verwendung von Keramik in den Burgen Lettlands
   vom 13.–16. Jahrhundert', *Castella Maris Baltici*, 14 (2021),
   pp. 9–18.

27 Christofer Herrmann, *Der Hochmeisterpalast auf der Marienbur:
   Konzeption, Bau und Nutzung der modernsten europäischen
   Fürstenresidenz um 1400* (Petersberg, 2019), pp. 517–18.

28 Kazimierz Pospieszny, *Malborksa rezydencja wielkich mistrzów, królów
   i cesarzy* (Malbork, 1991) p. 12.

29 Janusz Trupinda, '1.3.3. Zespół heraldyczny z herbem von Jungingen
   ok. 1400', in *Fundacje artystyczne na terenie Państwa Krzyżackiego
   w Prusach*, ed. Pospiezna, p. 85.

30 Jerzy Domasłowski, 'Krzyżacy, biskupi, mieszczanie . . . malowidła
   ścienne w panstwie zakonnym i krąg fundatowrów do połowy XV
   wieku', in *Fundacje artystyczne na terenie Państwa Krzyżackiego
   w Prusach*, ed. Pospiezna, pp. 106–41 (pp. 107 and 112).

31 Andrzej Woziński, 'Późnogotycka rzeźba w państwie zakonnym',
   in *Fundacje artystyczne na terenie Państwa Krzyżackiego w Prusach II*,
   ed. Pospieszna, pp. 195–212.

32 Marian Dygo, 'The Political Role of the Cult of the Virgin Mary
   in Teutonic Prussia in the Fourteenth and Fifteenth Centuries',
   Journal of Medieval History, xv/1 (1989), pp. 63–81 (p. 65).
33 Anna Błażejewska, '1.2.1. "Złota brama", k. xiii. w', in *Fundacje
   artystyczne na terenie Państwa Krzyżackiego w Prusach 1*, ed.
   Pospieszna, p. 19.
34 Kazimierz Pospieszny, '1.2.13. Główny zwornik z "madonną
   tronującą" z kościoła zamkowego w Malborku, ok. 1340', in
   Fundacje artystyczne na terenie Państwa Krzyżackiego w Prusach 1,
   ed. Pospieszna, pp. 35–6.
35 Dygo, 'The Political Role', p. 67.
36 Woziński, 'Późnogotycka rzeźba', p. 172.
37 Paweł Gancarczyk, 'Kultura muzyczna zakonu krzyżackiego
   w Prusach', in *Fundacje artystyczne na terenie Państwa Krzyżackiego
   w Prusach 1*, ed. Pospieszna, pp. 269–82 (p. 273).
38 For the latest study on the portal, see Bogna Jakubowska, *Magiczna
   przestrzeń złotej bramy w Malborku 2016* (Malbork, 2016).
39 Kazimierz Pospieszny, '1.2.11. Cegiełka fryzowa z lwem z zamku
   w Brandenburgu, ok. 1280', in *Fundacje artystyczne na terenie
   Państwa Krzyżackiego w Prusach 1*, ed. Pospieszna, p. 33.
40 Anna Błażejewksa, '11.5.3. Głowa św. Jana Chrzciciela na misie
   z kościoła cysterek w chełmnie, ok. 1380', in *Fundacje artystyczne
   na terenie Państwa Krzyżackiego w Prusach 1*, ed. Pospieszna, p. 176.
41 Jakubowska, *Magiczna przestrzeń*, pp. 314–58.
42 Domasłowski, 'Krzyżacy, biskupi, mieszczanie', p. 112.
43 Tadeusz Jurkowlaniec, 'Portale północny i południowy kalplicy Sw.
   Anny, ok. 1340', in *Fundacje artystyczne na terenie Państwa
   Krzyżackiego w Prusach 1*, ed. Pospieszna, pp. 54–6.
44 Herrmann, 'Kloster und Burg', p. 218.
45 Sven Ekdahl, 'The Strategic Organization of the Commanderies
   of the Teutonic Order in Prussia and Livonia', in *La Commanderie:
   Institution des ordres militaires dans l'Occident médiéval*, ed. Anthony
   Luttrell and L. Pressouyre (Paris, 2002), pp. 219–42 (p. 222).
46 Gancewski, *Rola zamków*, p. 77.
47 Ibid., p. 78.
48 Andrzej Nowakowski, *Arms and Armour in the Medieval Teutonic
   Order's State in Prussia* (Łódź, 1994), pp. 102–3.
49 Wojciech Brillowski and Arkadiusz Koperkiewicz, 'Analysis of Form
   and Function of Small Castle Architecture in the Eastern Part
   of the Teutonic Order's Lands', *Castella Maris Baltici*, 10 (2013),
   pp. 33–44.

50 Radosław Herman and Wojciech Dudak, 'Wyniki badań naukowych a projekt adaptacji zamku: Wzajemne uwarunkowania na przykładach zamków w Uniejowie, Lidzbarku i Ełku', in *Renovatio et restitutio: Materiały do badań i ochrony założeń rezydencjonalnych i obronnych*, ed. Piotr Lasek and Piotr Sypczuk (Warsaw, 2015), pp. 27–57.

51 Mieczysław Haftka, *Zamki krzyżackie w Polsce: Szkice z dziejów* (Malbork, 1999), pp. 215–17.

52 Martti Veldi, 'Roads and Hill Forts in Southern Estonia during the German Conquest in Henry's *Chronicle of Livonia*', in *Strongholds and Power Centres East of the Baltic Sea in the 11th–13th Centuries*, ed. Heiki Valk (Tartu, 2014), pp. 385–416.

53 Aleksander Pluskowski, Heiki Valk, Juhan Kreem and Gundars Kalniņš, 'Sites in Livonia: The Historical and Archaeological Background', in *Environment, Colonization and the Baltic Crusader States*, ed. Aleks Pluskowski (Turnhout, 2019), pp. 79–104.

54 On Narwa, see Villu Kadakas, 'Territorial Development of the Castle of Narva', in *Livland im Mittelalter: Geschichte und Architektur*, ed. Christofer Hermann and Birgit Aldenhoff (Petersberg, 2022), pp. 92–107.

7 Crusading in the Wilderness

1 *Chronicle* III:221; Sławomir Wyszomirski and Jarosław Wenta, trans., *Piotr z Dusburga, Kronika ziemi pruskiej* (Toruń, 2011).

2 Werner Paravicini, *Die Preußenreisen des europäischen Adels*, 3 vols (Sigmaringen, 1989–95; repr. Göttingen, 2020); Gregory Leighton, *Ideology and Holy Landscape in the Baltic Crusades* (Leeds, 2022).

3 Alan Murray, 'Contrasting Masculinities in the Baltic Crusades: Teutonic Knights and Secular Crusaders at War and Peace in Late Medieval Prussia', in *Crusading and Masculinities*, ed. Natasha Hodgson, Katherine Lewis and Matthew Mesley (London, 2019), pp. 113–28.

4 For the Order's indulgences in relation to Lithuania, see Axel Ehlers, *Die Ablasspraxis des Deutschen Ordens im Mittelalter* (Marburg, 2007), pp. 50–76, with full transcripts of the most important indulgences of the *Reise* on pp. 532–7, and for a summary, see Axel Ehlers, 'The Use of Indulgences by the Teutonic Order in the Middle Ages', in *The Military Orders*, vol. III: *History and Heritage*, ed. Victor Mallia-Milanes (Aldershot, 2008), pp. 139–45.

5 Marian Dygo, 'The Political Role of the Cult of the Virgin Mary in Teutonic Prussia in the Fourteenth and Fifteenth Centuries', *Journal of Medieval History*, xv/1 (1989), pp. 63–81 (p. 67); Antoni Chodyński, *Broń i barwa w czasach krzyżackich od XIII do połowy XVI wieku* (Malbork, 2003), p. 19.

6 Paul Milliman, *'The Slippery Memory of Men': The Place of Pomerania in the Medieval Kingdom of Poland* (Leiden, 2013), Appendix 3.

7 Hienadź Semiańczuk, 'Wiedza geograficzna w zakonie krzyżackim o ziemiach Białoruskich wielkiego Księstwa Litewskiego w XIV wieku', in *Kancelarie Krzyżackie: Stan badań i perspektywy badawcze*, ed. Janusz Trupinda (Malbork, 2002), pp. 225–34 (p. 227).

8 Anti Selart, *Livonia, Rus' and the Baltic Crusades in the Thirteenth Century* (Leiden, 2015), p. 278.

9 Anna Supruniuk, 'O wyprawach do Prus rycerczy polskich i wojnie domowej w koronie w latach 1382–1385', *Zapiski Historyczne*, 2 (2000), pp. 31–54 (pp. 32–3).

10 Timothy Guard, *Chivalry, Kingship and Crusade: The English Experience in the Fourteenth Century* (Woodbridge, 2016).

11 Albert Cook, 'Beginning the Board in Prussia', *Journal of English and Germanic Philology*, xiv/3 (1915), pp. 375–88 (p. 377).

12 Andrzej Nowakowski, *Arms and Armour in the Medieval Teutonic Order's State in Prussia* (Łódź, 1994), p. 34.

13 Tadeusz Jurkowlaniec, 'Z Prus do wieczności . . . o nagrobkach', in *Fundacje artystyczne na terenie Państwa Krzyżackiego w Prusach*, ed. Barbara Pospieszna (Pelplin, 2010), pp. 213–22 (p. 214).

14 On the biblical wilderness, see Corinne Saunders, *The Forest of Medieval Romance* (Cambridge, 1993); numerous examples of these terms used to describe the frontier can be found in Wigand of Marburg's *Chronicle*; see Theodor Hirsch, *Die Chronik Wigands von Marburg* (Leipzig, 1861; repr. Frankfurt am Main, 1965).

15 Jerzy Łapo, 'Rola Węgorzewa w systemie militarnym państwa krzyżackiego', in *Wojsko na Mazurach na przestrzeni dziejów: Wojsko na Ziemi Węgorzewskiej*, ed. Wiesław Łach (Węgorzewo, 2001), p. 33.

16 Grzegorz Białuński, *Kolonizacja Wielkiej Puszczy (do 1568 roku) – starostwa piskie, ełckie, starduńskie, zelkowski i węgoborskie (węgorzeweskie)* (Olsztyn, 2002), p. 13.

17 For a critique, see Krszysztof Kwiatkowski, 'Kapitulacje załóg punktów umocnionych w wojnach pruskiej gałęzi zakonu niemieckiego z Litwą od końca XIII do początku XV stulecia',

Kapitulacje w dziejach wojen: Z dziejów wojskowości polskiej i powszechnej, ed. Andrzej Niewiński (Oświęcim, 2017), pp. 117–58.

18 Jerzy Antoniewicz, 'Z zagadnień ochrony zabytków wczesnośredniowiecznego budownictwa obronnego na warmii i mazurach', *Sprawozdań PMA*, III/1–4 (1950), pp. 51–77 (pp. 60–64).

19 Arkadiusz Koperkiewicz, *Bezławki – ocalić od zniszczenia: Wyniki prac interdyscyplinarnych prowadzonych w latach, 2008–2011* (Gdańsk, 2013); for a critique, see Krzysztof Kwiatkowski, '(Wild)haus in Bezławki (Bayselauken, Bäslack): Remarks on the Construction of Fortifications of the Teutonic Order in Late Medieval Prussia', *Zapiski Historyczne*, LXXX/2 (2016), pp. 7–38.

20 Felix Biermann, Christofer Herrmann, Arkadiusz Koperkiewicz and Edvinas Ubis, 'Burning Alt-Wartenburg: Archaeological Evidence for the Conflicts between the Teutonic Order and the Grand Duchy of Lithuania from a Deserted Medieval Town near Barczewko (Warmia, Poland)', *Lietuvos Archeologija*, 45 (2019), pp. 265–93.

21 Białuński, *Kolonizacja Wielkiej Puszczy*, pp. 167–8.

22 Ibid., pp. 21–2.

23 Edvinas Ubis, 'Archaeological Data as Evidence of Cultural Interaction between the Teutonic Order and Local Communities: Problems and Perspectives', *Archaeologia Baltica*, 25 (2018), pp. 164–76 (pp. 171–2).

24 Vladas Žulkus, 'Der Hausbau in Klaipėda (Memel)', in *Lübecker Kolloquium zur Stadtarchäologie im Hanseraum III: der Hausbau*, ed. Brigitte Dahmen et al. (Lübeck, 2001), pp. 529–49; Vladas Žulkus, 'Die mittelalterliche und frühneuzeitliche Infrastuktur der Stadt Memel', in *Lübecker Kolloquium zur Stadtarchäologie im Hanseraum IV: die Infrastruktur*, ed. Regina Dunckel et al. (Lübeck, 2004), pp. 371–84.

25 Sławomir Jóźwiak and Janusz Trupinda, 'Budowa krzyżackiego zamku komturskiego w Ragnecie w końcu XIV–na początku XV wieku i jego układ przestrzenny', *Kwartalnik Historii Kultury Materialnej*, LVII/3–4 (2009), pp. 339–68.

26 For more details on the conflict with Lithuania, see Stephen Rowell, *Lithuania Ascending: A Pagan Empire within East-Central Europe, 1295–1345* (Cambridge, 1994); William Urban, *The Last Years of the Teutonic Knights: Lithuania, Poland and the Teutonic Order* (Barnsley, 2019).

27 Rasa Mažeika and Loïc Chollet, 'Familiar Marvels? French and German Crusaders and Chroniclers Confront Baltic Pagan

Religions', *Francia: Forschungen zur westeuropäischen Geschichte*, XLIII (2016), pp. 41–62 (p. 48).

28 Lee Manion, 'Thinking through the English Crusading Romance: *Sir Gowther* and the Baltic', in *Thinking Medieval Romance*, ed. Katherine Little and Nicola McDonald (Oxford, 2018), pp. 68–90 (pp. 79–80).

8 Defeat and Decline in the Fifteenth Century

1 Sławomir Jóźwiak, 'Kryzys władzy terytorialnej', in *Państwo zakonu krzyżackiego w Prusach: Władza i społeczeństwo*, ed. Marian Biskup et al. (Warsaw, 2009), pp. 332–56 (pp. 332–3).

2 Janusz Tandecki, 'Zakon krzyżacki', in *Państwo zakonu krzyżackiego w Prusach*, ed. Biskup et al., pp. 405–19 (pp. 414–15).

3 Udo Arnold, 'Eight Hundred Years of the Teutonic Order', in *The Military Orders*, vol. I: *Fighting for the Faith and Caring for the Sick*, ed. Malcolm Barber (Aldershot, 1994), pp. 223–35.

4 Jürgen Sarnowsky, *Die Wirtschaftsführung des Deutschen Ordens in Preußen (1382–1454)* (Cologne, 1993).

5 For recent work on the battle, see Sven Ekdahl, 'Battlefield Archaeology at Grunwald (Tannenberg, Žalgiris): A Polish-Scandinavian Research Project during the Period 2014–2017', *Przegląd Historyczny*, CIX/2 (2018), pp. 239–66; Sven Ekdahl, 'Different Points of View on the Battle of Grunwald/Tannenberg 1410 from Poland and Germany and Their Roots in Handwritten and Printed Traditions', *Badań nad Książką i Księgozbiorami Historycznymi*, 13 (2019), pp. 41–65; Sławomir Jóźwiak, 'Review of Research on the Battle of Grunwald (15th July 1410) in Historical Studies over the Past Half-Century', *Quaestiones Medii Aevi Novae*, 18 (2013), pp. 281–301; Krzysztof Kwiatkowski, 'New Research into the Battle of Grunwald/Tannenberg/Žalgiris: Attempt at an Overview', *Roczniki Historyczne*, 79 (2013), pp. 1–31.

6 Zenon Nowak, 'Czy Prusy Krzyżackie były państwem nowożytnym?', in *Architectura et historia*, ed. Michał Woźniak (Toruń, 1999), pp. 79–89 (p. 84).

7 Grzegorz Białuski, *Kolonizacja Wielkiej Puszczy (do 1568 roku) – starostwa piskie, ełckie, starduńskie, zelkowskie i węgoborskie (węgorzeweskie)* (Olsztyn, 2002), p. 10.

8 Sławomir Jóźwiak, 'Rycerstwo-szlachta', in *Państwo zakonu krzyżackiego w Prusach*, ed. Biskup et al., pp. 450–59 (p. 455).

9 Andris Šnē, 'The Medieval Peasantry: On the Social and Religious Position of the Rural Natives in Southern Livonia (13th–15th Centuries)', *Ajalooline Ajakiri*, 1/2 (2008), pp. 89–100 (p. 94).

10 Roman Czaja, 'Die Entwicklung der ständischen Versammlungen in Livland, Preußen und Polen im Spätmittelalter', *Zeitschrift für Ostmitteleuropa-Forschung*, 3 (2009), pp. 312–28.

11 Pärtel Piirimäe, 'Staatenbund oder Ständestaat? Der livländische Landtag im Zeitalter Wolters von Plettenberg (1494–1535)', *Forschungen zur Baltischen Geschichte*, 8 (2013), pp. 40–80.

12 Adam Soćko, *Układy emporowe w architekturze państwa krzyżeackiego* (Warsaw, 2005), p. 115.

13 Beata Możejko, Dariusz Kaczor and Błażej śliwiński, 'Zarys dziejów klasztoru Dominikańskiego w Gdańsku od średniowiecza do czasów nowożytnych (1226/1227–1835)', *Archeologia Gdańska*, 1 (2006), pp. 137–214 (p. 172).

14 Antoni Czacharowski, 'Toruń średniowieczny (do roku 1454)', in *Toruń dawny i dzisiejszy: zarys dziejów*, ed. Marian Biskup (Warsaw, 1983), pp. 31–131 (p. 111).

15 Johannes Mol, 'The Knight Brothers from the Low Countries in the Conflict between the Westphalians and the Rhinelanders in the Livonian Branch of the Teutonic Order', *Ordines Militares*, 20 (2015), pp. 123–44.

16 Juhan Kreem, *The Town and Its Lord: Reval and the Teutonic Order (in the Fifteenth Century)* (Tallinn, 2002), p. 156.

17 Ibid., p. 159.

18 Ibid., p. 33.

19 Stephen Rowell, 'The Lithuano-Prussian Forest Frontier, c. 1422–1600', in *Frontiers in Question: Eurasian Borderlands, 700–1700*, ed. Daniel Power and Naomi Standen (Basingstoke, 1999), pp. 182–208 (pp. 190–91).

20 Jóźwiak, 'Rycerstwo-szlachta', p. 458.

21 Jóźwiak, 'Kryzys władzy terytorialnej', pp. 332–3.

9 The Reformation and the End of the Teutonic Order's Rule in the Baltic

1 Bernhart Jähnig, 'Albert de Brandebourg-Ansbach et la sécularisation de l'Ordre teutonique en Prusse', *Histoire, économie et société*, XXXII/2 (2013), pp. 19–27.

2 Udo Arnold, 'Hochmeister Albrecht von Brandenburg-Ansbach und Landmeister Gotthard Kettler: Ordensritter und

Territorialherren am Scheideweg in Preußen und Livland', in *The Military Orders and the Reformation: Choices, State Building, and the Weight of Tradition*, ed. Johannes A. Mol, Klaus Militzer and Helen J. Nicholson (Hilversum, 2006), pp. 11–29.

3 For the life of Albert, see also Walther Hubatsch, *Albrecht von Brandenburg-Ansbach, Deutschordens-Hochmeister und Herzog in Preußen, 1490–1568* (Cologne, 1965).

4 Mol, Militzer and Nicholson, eds, *The Military Orders and the Reformation*.

5 David Gaimster, 'Tile-Stove Production in the Baltic, c. 1400–1600: An Index of Hanseatic Cultural and Technological Exchange', in *Medieval Europe Basel: Centre, Region, Periphery: 3rd International Conference of Medieval and Later Archaeology, Basel 2002*, ed. Guido Helmig, Barbara Scholkmann and Matthias Untermann (Basel, 2002), pp. 110–17 (p. 114).

6 Stephen Rowell, 'The Lithuano-Prussian Forest Frontier, c. 1422–1600', in *Frontiers in Question: Eurasian Borderlands, 700–1700*, ed. Daniel Power and Naomi Standen (Basingstoke, 1999), pp. 182–208 (p. 195).

7 Borys Paszkiweicz, *Brakteaty – pieniądz średniowiecznych Prus* (Wrocław, 2009), pp. 240–48.

8 Ieva Masiulienė, '16th–17th Century Klaipėda Town Residents' Lifestyle', *Archaeologia Baltica*, 12 (2009), pp. 95–111.

9 Rowell, 'The Lithuano-Prussian Forest Frontier', p. 191.

10 Mieczysław Haftka, *Zamki krzyżackie w Polsce: Szkice z dziejów* (Malbork, 1999), p. 104.

11 Juhan Kreem, 'Der Deutsche Orden und die Reformation in Livland', in *The Military Orders and the Reformation*, ed. Mol, Militzer and Nicholson, pp. 43–57.

12 Kreem, 'Der Deutsche Orden', p. 47.

13 Juhan Kreem, 'Crusading Traditions and Chivalric Ideals: The Mentality of the Teutonic Order in Livonia at the Beginning of the Sixteenth Century', *Crusades*, xii/1 (2013), pp. 233–50.

14 Kreem, 'Der Deutsche Orden', pp. 50–51.

15 Johannes Mol, 'Traitor to Livonia? The Teutonic Order's Land Marshal Jasper van Munster', *Ordines Militares*, 19 (2015), pp. 205–40.

16 Arnold, 'Hochmeister Albrecht', p. 24.

17 Ulrich Schoenborn, 'Kurland im Horizont der Reformation: Resonanz – Korrelation – Interaktion', in *The Reformation in the Southeast Baltic Region/ Reformacija Baltijos jūros pietryčių regione*,

    ed. Arūnas Baublys and Vasilijus Safronovas (Klaipėda, 2017), pp. 45–82.

18 Jörg Seiler, 'Daß der Teutsch Orden noch nit erloschen . . .: strukturelle Wandlungen des deutschen Ordens im Reich im Gefolge der Reformation', in *The Military Orders and the Reformation*, ed. Mol, Militzer and Nicholson, pp. 139–80.

19 Johannes A. Mol, 'Trying to Survive: The Military Orders in Utrecht, 1580–1620', in *The Military Orders and the Reformation*, ed. Mol, Militzer and Nicholson, pp. 181–207.

10 The Rise and Fall of a Medieval Religious Corporation

 1 Udo Arnold, 'Eight Hundred Years of the Teutonic Order', in *The Military Orders*, vol. I: *Fighting for the Faith and Caring for the Sick*, ed. Malcolm Barber (Aldershot, 1994), pp. 223–35 (p. 226).

BIBLIOGRAPHY

Primary Sources

Brundage, James, trans., *The Chronicle of Henry of Livonia*
(New York, 2003)

Fischer, Mary, ed., *The Chronicle of Prussia by Nicolaus von Jeroschin:
A History of the Teutonic Knights in Prussia, 1190–1331*
(Farnham, 2010)

Hirsch, Theodor, trans., *Die Chronik Wigands von Marburg*
(Leipzig, 1861; repr. Frankfurt am Main, 1965)

Loud, Graham A., ed., *The Crusade of Frederick Barbarossa:
The History of the Expedition of the Emperor Frederick and
Related Texts* (London, 2010)

Smith, Jerry, and William Urban, trans., *The Livonian Rhymed
Chronicle* (London, 2017)

Šterns, Indriķis, trans., 'The Rule and Statutes of the Teutonic
Knights', *The Orb*, https://the-orb.arlima.net, accessed
7 January 2023

Wyszomirski, Sławomir, and Jarosław Wenta, trans., *Piotr
z Dusburga, Kronika ziemi pruskiej* (Toruń, 2011)

Ziesemer, Walther, ed., *Das gross Ämterbuch des deutschen
Ordens: Mit Unterstützung des Vereins für die Herstellung und
Ausschmückung der Marienburg* (Wiesbaden, 1968; repr. 2009)

Zimmermann, Franz, and Carl Werner, eds, *Urkundenbuch
zur Geschichte der Deutschen in Siebenbürgen*, vol. 1
(Hermannstadt, 1892)

Secondary Sources

Alttoa, Kaur, 'On the Architecture of Viljandi Castle', in *Viljandi
ordulinnus ja Lossimäed läbi aegade* (*The Teutonic Order's Castle and
Castle Hills in Viljandi through Time*), ed. Viljandi Museum (Viljandi,
2015), pp. 87–110 (Estonian and English)

Antoniewicz, Jerzy, 'Z zagadnień ochrony zabytków
wczesnośredniowiecznego budownictwa obronnego na warmii
i mazurach', *Sprawozdań PMA*, III/1–4 (1950), pp. 51–77

Arnold, Udo, 'Eight Hundred Years of the Teutonic Order', in
      The Military Orders, vol. i: *Fighting for the Faith and Caring for the
      Sick*, ed. Malcolm Barber (Aldershot, 1994), pp. 223–35
—, 'Hochmeister Albrecht von Brandenburg-Ansbach und Landmeister
      Gotthard Kettler', in *The Military Orders and the Reformation*,
      ed. Johannes A. Mol, Klaus Militzer and Helen J. Nicholson
      (Hilversum, 2006), pp. 11–29
Arszyński, Marian, *Budownictwo warowne zakonu krzyżackiego w Prusach*
      (1230–1454) (Toruń, 1995)
—, 'Architektura warowna Zakonu Krzyżackiego w Prusach', in *Fundacje*
      artystyczne na terenie państwa krzyżackiego w prusach, ed. Barbara
      Pospieszna (Pelplin, 2010), pp. 7–45
—, 'Zamki i umocnienia zakonu krzyżackiego i biskupów w inflantach',
      in *Zakon krzyżacki w Prusach i Inflantach: podziały administracyjne*
      i kościelne w XIII–XVI wieku, ed. Roman Czaja and Andrzej
      Radzimiński (Toruń, 2013), pp. 183–213
Asbridge, Thomas, *The Crusades: The War for the Holy Land*
      (London, 2010)
—, *The First Crusade: A New History* (London, 2012)
Aubin, Hermann, 'The Lands East of the Elbe and German Colonization
      Eastwards', in *The Cambridge Economic History of Europe from the*
      Decline of the Roman Empire, vol. i: *Agrarian Life of the Middle Ages*,
      ed. Michael M. Postan (Cambridge, 1966), pp. 449–86
Auns, Muntis, 'Acquisition of the Acquired: The Establishing of a
      Real Administration in Livonia', in *Culture Clash or Compromise?*
      The Europeanisation of the Baltic Sea Area, 1100–1400 AD, ed. Nils
      Blomkvist (Visby, 1998), pp. 259–67
Barber, Malcolm, *The Crusader States* (New Haven, CT, 2012)
Białuński, Grzegorz, *Osadnictwo regionu Wielkich Jezior Mazurskich*
      od XIV do początku XVIII wieku – starostwo leckie (giżyckie) i ryńskie
      (Olsztyn, 1996)
—, *Studia z dziejów plemion pruskich i jaćwieskich* (Olsztyn, 1999)
—, *Przemiany społeczno-ludnościowe południowo-wschodnich obszarów*
      Prus Krzyżackich i Książęcych (do 1568 roku)(Olsztyn, 2001)
—, *Kolonizacja Wielkiej Puszczy (do 1568 roku) – starostwa piskie,*
      ełckie, starduńskie, zelkowski i węgoborskie (węgorzeweskie)
      (Olsztyn, 2002)
Biermann, Felix, Christofer Herrmann, Arkadiusz Koperkiewicz
      and Edvinas Ubis, 'Burning Alt-Wartenburg: Archaeological
      Evidence for the Conflicts between the Teutonic Order and the
      Grand Duchy of Lithuania from a Deserted Medieval Town near

Barczewko (Warmia, Poland)', *Lietuvos Archeologija*, 45 (2019), pp. 265–93

Biskup, Marian, 'Bemerkungen zum Siedlungsproblem und den Pfarrbezirken in Ordenspreussen im 14–15 Jahrhundert', in *Die Rolle der Ritterorden in der Christianisierung und Kolonisierung des Ostseegebietes*, ed. Zenon Nowak (Toruń, 1983), pp. 35–56

——, 'Etniczno-demograficzne przemiany Prus Krzyżackich w rozwoju osadnictwa w średniowieczu', in *Opera Minora: Studia z dziejów zakonu Krzyżackiego* (Toruń, 2002), pp. 129–50

Błażejewska, Anna, '1.2.1. "Złota brama", k. XIII. w', in *Fundacje artystyczne na terenie Państwa Krzyżackiego w Prusach I*, ed. Barbara Pospieszna (Pelplin, 2010), p. 19

Boas, Adrian, *Archaeology of the Military Orders: A Survey of the Urban Centres, Rural Settlements and Castles of the Military Orders in the Latin East (c. 1120–1291)* (London, 2006)

——, and Rabei Khamisy, eds, *Montfort: History, Early Research and Recent Studies of the Principal Fortress of the Teutonic Order in the Latin East* (Leiden, 2017)

——, and Georg Melloni, 'New Evidence for Identifying the Site of the Teutonic Compound in Acre', in *Acre and Its Falls: Studies in the History of a Crusader City*, ed. John France (Leiden, 2018), pp. 69–89

Bom, Myra Miranda, *Women in the Military Orders of the Crusades* (New York, 2012)

Borchardt, Karl, 'Late Medieval Indulgences for the Hospitallers and the Teutonic Order', *Ablasskampagnen des Spätmittelalters: Luthers Thesen von 1517 im Kontext*, ed. Andreas Rehberg (Berlin, 2017), pp. 195–218

Brillowski, Wojciech, and Arkadiusz Koperkiewicz, 'Analysis of Form and Function of Small Castle Architecture in the Eastern Part of the Teutonic Order's Lands', *Castella Maris Baltici*, 10 (2013), pp. 33–44

Caune, Andris, and Ieva Ose, *Latvijas 12. gadsimta beigu – 17. gadsimta vācu piļu leksikons* (Riga, 2004)

Chodyński, Antoni, *Broń i barwa w czasach krzyżackich od XIII do połowy XVI wieku* (Malbork, 2003)

Christiansen, Eric, *The Northern Crusades* (London, 1997)

Chruścińska, Alicja, Bernard Jesionowski, Hubert Oczkowski and Krzysztof Przegiętka, 'Using the TL Single-Aliquot Regenerative-Dose Protocol for the Verification of the Chronology of the Teutonic Order Castle in Malbork', *Geochronometria*, XXX/1 (2008), pp. 61–7

Chudziak, Wojeciech, *Wczesnośredniowieczna przestrzeń sakralna in Culmine na Pomorzu Nadwiślańskim* (Toruń, 2003)

—, and Jacek Bojarski, 'Chełmno i Toruń: Początki miast na ziemi chełmińskiej', *Archaeologia Historica Polona*, XXIII/83 (2015), pp. 83–105 (90–99)

Cook, Albert, 'Beginning the Board in Prussia', *Journal of English and Germanic Philology*, XIV/3 (1915), pp. 375–88

Czacharowski, Antoni, 'Toruń średniowieczny (do roku 1454)', in *Toruń dawny i dzisiejszy: Zarys dziejów*, ed. Marian Biskup (Warsaw, 1983), pp. 31–131

Czaja, Roman, 'Die Entwicklung der ständischen Versammlungen in Livland, Preußen und Polen im Spätmittelalter', *Zeitschrift für Ostmitteleuropa-Forschung*, 3 (2009), pp. 312–28

—, 'Rozwój osadnictwa miejskiego', in *Państwo zakonu krzyżackiego w Prusach: Władza i społeczeństwo*, ed. Marian Biskup et al., (Warsaw, 2009), pp. 370–83

—, 'Urbanizacja kraju', in *Państwo zakonu krzyżackiego w Prusach: Władza i społeczeństwo*, ed. Marian Biskup et al. (Warsaw, 2009), pp. 177–230

—, 'Miasta inflanckie XIII–XVI w', in *Zakon krzyżacki w Prusach i Inflantach: podziały administracyjne i kościelne w XIII–XVI wieku*, ed. Roman Czaja and Andrzej Radzimiński (Toruń, 2013), pp. 215–40

—, and Zenon Nowak, 'Państwo zakonu krzyżackiego w prusach – próba charakterystyki', in *Zakon krzyżacki w Prusach i Inflantach: podziały administracyjne i kościelne w XIII–XVI wieku*, ed. Roman Czaja and Andrzej Radzimiński (Toruń, 2013), pp. 1–27

—, and Andrzej Radzimiński, eds, *Zakon krzyżacki w Prusach i Inflantach: podziały administracyjne i kościelne w XIII–XVI wieku* (Toruń, 2013)

Długokęcki, Wiesław, 'Kolonizacja ziemi chełmińskiej, Prus i Pomorza Gdańskiego do 1410 r.', in *Państwo zakonu krzyżackiego w Prusach: Władza i społeczeństwo*, ed. Marian Biskup et al. (Warsaw, 2009), pp. 200–217

—, 'Społeczeństwo wiejskie', in *Państwo zakonu krzyżackiego w Prusach: Władza i społeczeństwo*, ed. Marian Biskup et al. (Warsaw, 2009) pp. 460–94

Domasłowski, Jerzy, 'Krzyżacy, biskupi, mieszczanie . . . malowidła ścienne w panstwie zakonnym i krąg fundatowrów do połowy XV wieku', in *Fundacje artystyczne na terenie Państwa Krzyżackiego w Prusach*, ed. Barbara Pospiezna (Pelplin, 2010), pp. 106–41

Dygo, Marian, 'The Political Role of the Cult of the Virgin Mary
    in Teutonic Prussia in the Fourteenth and Fifteenth Centuries',
    Journal of Medieval History, xv/1 (1989), pp. 63–80
——, 'Początki i budowa władztwa zakonu krzyżackiego (1226–1309)',
    in *Państwo zakonu krzyżackiego w Prusach: Władza i społeczeństwo*,
    ed. Marian Biskup et al. (Warsaw, 2009), pp. 53–78
Ehlers, Axel, 'The Crusade against Lithuania Reconsidered', in *Crusade
    and Conversion on the Baltic Frontier, 1150–1500*, ed. Alan V. Murray
    (Farnham, 2001), pp. 21–44
——, *Die Ablasspraxis des Deutschen Ordens im Mittelalter* (Marburg, 2007)
——, 'The Use of Indulgences by the Teutonic Order in the Middle Ages',
    in *The Military Orders*, vol. iii: *History and Heritage*, ed. Victor
    Mallia-Milanes (Aldershot, 2008), pp. 139–45
Eihmane, Eva, 'The Baltic Crusades: A Clash of Two Identities', in
    The Clash of Cultures on the Medieval Baltic Frontier, ed. Alan V.
    Murray (Farnham, 2009), pp. 37–52
——, 'Livonia and the Holy See in 13th–Early 15th Centuries:
    Centre and Periphery of Christendom', in *The Image of the Baltic:
    A Festschrift for Nils Blomkvist*, ed. Michael Scholz, Robert Bohn
    and Carina Johansson (Visby, 2012), pp. 23–40
Ekdahl, Sven, 'Horses and Crossbows: Two Important Warfare
    Advantages of the Teutonic Order in Prussia', in *The Military Orders*,
    vol. ii: *Welfare and Warfare*, ed. Helen Nicholson (Farnham, 1998),
    pp. 119–51
——, 'The Strategic Organization of the Commanderies of the Teutonic
    Order in Prussia and Livonia', in *La Commanderie: Institution des
    ordres militaires dans l'Occident médiéval*, ed. Anthony Luttrell and
    L. Pressouyre (Paris, 2002), pp. 219–42
——, 'Battlefield Archaeology at Grunwald (Tannenberg, Žalgiris):
    A Polish-Scandinavian Research Project during the Period
    2014–2017', *Przegląd Historyczny*, cix/2 (2018), pp. 239–66
——, 'Different Points of View on the Battle of Grunwald/Tannenberg
    1410 from Poland and Germany and Their Roots in Handwritten
    and Printed Traditions', *Badań nad Książką i Księgozbiorami
    Historycznymi*, 13 (2019), pp. 41–65
Fonnesberg-Schmidt, Iben, *The Popes and the Baltic Crusades,
    1147–1254* (Leiden, 2007)
Frycz, Jerzy, 'Architektura zamków krzyżackich', in *Sztuka pobrzeża
    Bałtyku*, ed. Hanna Fruba (Warsaw, 1978), pp. 19–43
Gaimster, David, 'Tile-Stove Production in the Baltic, c. 1400–1600: An
    Index of Hanseatic Cultural and Technological Exchange', in *Medieval*

*Europe Basel: Centre, Region, Periphery: 3rd International Conference
    of Medieval and Later Archaeology, Basel 2002*, ed. Guido Helmig,
    Barbara Scholkmann and Matthias Untermann (Basel, 2002),
    pp. 110–17

Gancarczyk, Paweł, 'Kultura muzyczna zakonu krzyżackiego w Prusach',
    in *Fundacje artystyczne na terenie Państwa Krzyżackiego w Prusach*,
    ed. Barbara Pospieszna (Pelplin, 2010), pp. 269–82

Gancewski, Jan, *Rola zamków krzyżackich w ziemi chelminskiej od polowy
    xiv wieku do 1454 roku* (Olsztyn, 2001)

Gazda, Daniel, ed., *Wielokulturowy obiekt warowny na Górze
    Zamkowej oraz gród cyplowy w Starym Dzierzgoniu: studia i materialy*
    (Warsaw, 2018)

Gouguenheim, Sylvain, *Krzyżacy* (Malbork, 2012)

Guard, Timothy, *Chivalry, Kingship and Crusade: The English Experience
    in the Fourteenth Century* (Woodbridge, 2016)

Haak, Arvi, 'Archaeological Data about the Viljandi Castle in the
    Medieval and Early Modern Period', in *Viljandi ordulinnus ja
    Lossimäed läbi aegade (The Teutonic Order's Castle and Castle Hills in
    Viljandi through Time)*, ed. Viljandi Museum (Viljandi, 2015),
    pp. 27–64 (Estonian and English)

Haftka, Mieczysław, *Zamki krzyżackie w Polsce: Szkice z dziejów* (Malbork,
    1999)

Herman, Radosław, and Wojciech Dudak, 'Wyniki badań naukowych a
    projekt adaptacji zamku: Wzajemne uwarunkowania na przykładach
    zamków w Uniejowie, Lidzbarku i Ełku', in *Renovatio et restitutio:
    Materiały do badań i ochrony założeń rezydencjonalnych i obronnych*,
    ed. Piotr Lasek and Piotr Sypczuk (Warsaw, 2015), pp. 27–57

Herrmann, Christofer, *Mittelalterliche Architektur in Preussenland:
    Untersuchungen zur Frage der Kunstlandschaft und -geographie*
    (Petersberg, 2007)

——, 'Kloster und Burg: die Architektur des Deutschen Ordens in Preußen
    und Livlan', in *Glaube, Macht und Pracht: Geistliche Gemeinschaften
    des Ostseeraums im Zeitalter der Backsteingotik*, ed. Oliver Auge, Felix
    Biermann und Christofer Herrmann (Rahden, 2009), pp. 209–20

——, *Der Hochmeisterpalast auf der Marienburg: Konzeption, Bau und
    Nutzung der modernsten europäischen Fürstenresidenz um 1400*
    (Petersberg, 2019)

Hubatsch, Walther, *Albrecht von Brandenburg-Ansbach, Deutschordens-
    Hochmeister und Herzog in Preußen, 1490–1568* (Cologne, 1965)

Hunyadi, Zsolt, 'The Teutonic Order in Burzenland (1211–1225): New
    Re-Considerations', in *L'Ordine Teutonico tra Mediterraneo e Baltico:*

Incontri e scontri tra religioni, popoli e culture, ed. Hubert Houben and
Kristjan Toomaspoeg (Galatina, 2008), pp. 151–62

Ionita, Adrian, *Feldioara-Marienburg: contributii arheologice la istoria Ţării
Bârsei* (Bucharest, 2004)

Jähnig, Bernhart, 'Albert de Brandebourg-Ansbach et la sécularisation
de l'Ordre teutonique en Prusse', *Histoire, économie et société*, xxxii/2
(2013), pp. 19–27

Jakubowska, Bogna, *Magiczna przestrzeńzłotej bramy w Malborku*
(Malbork, 2016)

Jarockis, Romas, 'Semigallia, 1100–1400: A Review of Archaeological
and Historical Sources', in *Culture Clash or Compromise? The
Europeanisation of the Baltic Sea Area, 1100–1400 AD*, ed. Nils
Blomkvist (Visby, 1998), pp. 45–53

Jesionowski, Bernard, 'Dzieje budowlane skrzydła zachodniego w świetle
obserwacji architektonicznych', in *Wileki refektarz na zamku średnim
w Malborku: dzieje – wstrój – konserwacja*, ed. Janusz Trupinda
(Malbork, 2010), pp. 13–30

Jotischky, Andrew, *Crusading and the Crusader States* (London, 2017)

Jóźwiak, Sławomir, *Centralne i terytorialne organy władzy zakonu
krzyżackiego w Prusach w latach 1228–1410: rozwój, przekształcenia,
kompetencje* (Toruń, 2001)

——, 'Kryzys władzy terytorialnej', in *Państwo zakonu krzyżeackiego
w Prusach: Władza i społeczeństwo*, ed. Marian Biskup et al.
(Warsaw, 2009), pp. 332–56

——, 'Podziały administracyjne', in *Państwo zakonu krzyżackiego w Prusach:
Władza i społeczeństwo*, ed. Marian Biskup et al. (Warsaw, 2009),
pp. 132–7

——, 'Rycerstwo-szlachta', in *Państwo zakonu krzyżackiego w Prusach:
Władza i społeczeństwo*, ed. Marian Biskup et al. (Warsaw, 2009),
pp. 450–59

——, 'Organizacja życia na zamku krzyżackim w późnym średniowieczu
na przykładzie stołecznej warowni malborskiej', in *Sapientia
aedificavit sibi domum*, ed. Janusz Trupinda (Malbork, 2019),
pp. 288–310

Joźwiak, Sławomir, and Janusz Trupinda, *Organizacja żeycia na zamku
krzyżeackim w Malborku w czasach wielkich mistrzoźw (1309–1457)*
(Malbork, 2007)

——, 'Budowa krzyżackiego zamku komturskiego w Ragnecie w końcu
xiv–na początku xv wieku i jego układ przestrzenny', *Kwartalnik
Historii Kultury Materialnej*, lvii/3–4 (2009), pp. 339–68

——, *Krzyżackie zamki komturskie w Prusach* (Toruń, 2012)

——, 'Review of Research on the Battle of Grunwald (15th July 1410)
in Historical Studies over the Past Half-Century', *Quaestiones
Medii Aevi Novae*, 18 (2013), pp. 281–301

——, 'Czy rzeczywiście wbrew "tradycji"? O współczesnych badaniach
nad zamkami krzyżackimi na tle ustaleń historiografii z XIX i I.
połowy XX wieku', *Archaeologia Historica Polona*, 26 (2018),
pp. 25–39

Jurkowlaniec, Tadeusz, 'Portale północny i południowy kalplicy Sw. Anny,
ok. 1340', in *Fundacje artystyczne na terenie Państwa Krzyżackiego
w Prusach I*, ed. Barbara Pospieszna (Pelplin, 2010), pp. 54–6

——, 'Z Prus do wieczności . . . o nagrobkach', in *Fundacje artystyczne
na terenie Państwa Krzyżackiego w Prusach*, ed. Barbara Pospieszna
(Pelplin, 2010), pp. 213–22

Khamisy, Rabei, 'Archaeological Remains of the 1202 Earthquake
in the Frankish Village of Tarphile/Khirbat al-Manḥata', *Levant*,
XCIX/3 (2017), pp. 333–41

Kochański, Rafał, 'Fosy i mosty jako element obronności zamków
krzyżackich w Prusach', *Materiały Zachodniopomorskie*, 46 (2001),
pp. 457–81

Koperkiewicz, Arkadiusz, *Bezławki – ocalić od zniszczenia: Wyniki prac
interdyscyplinarnych prowadzonych w latach 2008–2011* (Gdańsk,
2013)

Kreem, Juhan, 'The Teutonic Order as a Secular Ruler in Livonia:
The Privileges and Oath of Reval', in *Crusade and Conversion
on the Baltic Frontier, 1150–1500*, ed. Alan V. Murray (Farnham,
2001), pp. 215–32

——, *The Town and Its Lord: Reval and the Teutonic Order (in the Fifteenth
Century)* (Tallinn, 2002)

——, 'Der Deutsche Orden und die Reformation in Livland', in *The
Military Orders and the Reformation*, ed. Johannes A. Mol, Klaus
Militzer and Helen J. Nicholson (Hilversum, 2006), pp. 43–57

——, 'Mobility of the Livonian Teutonic Knights', in *Making Livonia:
Actors and Networks in the Medieval and Early Modern Baltic Sea
Region*, ed. Anu Mänd and Marek Tamm (London, 2020),
pp. 158–69

Kwiatkowski, Krszysztof, 'New Research into the Battle of Grunwald/
Tannenberg/Žalgiris Attempt at an Overview', *Roczniki Historyczne*,
79 (2013), pp. 1–31

——, '(Wild)haus in Bezławki (Bayselauken, Bäslack): Remarks on
the Construction of Fortifications of the Teutonic Order in Late
Medieval Prussia', *Zapiski Historyczne*, LXXX/2 (2016), pp. 7–38

——, 'Kapitulacje załóg punktów umocnionych w wojnach pruskiej
    gałęzi zakonu niemieckiego z Litwą od końca XIII do początku
    XV stulecia', *Kapitulacje w dziejach wojen: Z dziejów wojskowości
    polskiej i powszechnej*, ed. Andrzej Niewiński (Oświęcim, 2017),
    pp. 117–58

Lang, Valter, and Heiki Valk, 'An Archaeological Reading of
    the Chronicle of Henry of Livonia: Traces, Contexts and
    Interpretations', in *Crusading and Chronicle Writing on the Medieval
    Baltic Frontier: A Companion to the Chronicle of Henry of Livonia*,
    ed. Marek Tamm, Linda Kaljundi and Carsten Selch Jensen
    (Farnham, 2011), pp. 291–316

Łapo, Jerzy, 'Rola Węgorzewa w systemie militarnym państwa
    krzyżackiego', in *Wojsko na Mazurach na przestrzeni dziejów: Wojsko
    na Ziemi Węgorzewskiej*, ed. Wiesław Łach (Węgorzewo, 2001),
    p. 33

Laszlovszky, József, and Zóltan Soós, 'Historical Monuments of the
    Teutonic Order in Transylvania', in *The Crusades and the Military
    Orders*, ed. Zsolt Hunyadi and József Laszlovszky (Budapest, 2001),
    pp. 319–36

Leighton, Gregory, *Ideology and Holy Landscape in the Baltic Crusades*
    (Leeds, 2022)

Luttrell, Anthony, 'The Hospitaller Background of the Teutonic Order',
    Ordines Militares, 26 (2021), pp. 351–75

Mänd, Anu, 'Saints' Cults in Medieval Livonia', in *The Clash of Cultures
    on the Medieval Baltic Frontier*, ed. Alan V. Murray (Farnham, 2009),
    pp. 191–223

Manion, Lee, 'Thinking through the English Crusading Romance:
    Sir Gowther and the Baltic', in *Thinking Medieval Romance*,
    ed. Katherine Little and Nicola McDonald (Oxford, 2018),
    pp. 68–90

Masiulienė, Ieva, '16th–17th Century Klaipėda Town Residents'
    Lifestyle', *Archaeologia Baltica*, 12 (2009), pp. 95–111

Mažeika, Rasa, and Loïc Chollet, 'Familiar Marvels? French and
    German Crusaders and Chroniclers Confront Baltic Pagan
    Religions', *Francia: Forschungen zur westeuropäischen Geschichte*,
    XLIII (2016), pp. 41–62

Militzer, Klaus, *Die Entstehung der Deutschordensballeien im Deutschen
    Reich* (Marburg, 1981)

——, 'The Role of Hospitals in the Teutonic Order', in *The Military
    Orders*, vol. II: *Welfare and Warfare*, ed. Helen Nicholson (London,
    1998), pp. 51–9

Milliman, Paul, 'The Slippery Memory of Men': The Place of Pomerania in
    the Medieval Kingdom of Poland (Leiden, 2013)
Mol, Johannes, 'Trying to Survive: The Military Orders in Utrecht,
    1580–1620', in The Military Orders and the Reformation, ed. Johannes
    A. Mol, Klaus Militzer and Helen J. Nicholson (Hilversum, 2006),
    pp. 181–207
—, 'The Knight Brothers from the Low Countries in the Conflict
    between the Westphalians and the Rhinelanders in the Livonian
    Branch of the Teutonic Order', Ordines Militares, 20 (2015),
    pp. 123–44
—, 'Traitor to Livonia? The Teutonic Order's Land Marshal Jasper van
    Munster', Ordines Militares, 19 (2015), pp. 205–40
—, Klaus Militzer and Helen Nicholson, eds, The Military Orders and
    the Reformation: Choices, State Building, and the Weight of Tradition
    (Hilversum, 2006)
Morton, Nicholas, The Teutonic Knights in the Holy Land, 1190–1291
    (Woodbridge, 2009)
Możejko, Beata, Dariusz Kaczor and Błażej Śliwiński, 'Zarys dziejów
    klasztoru Dominikańskiego w Gdańsku od średniowiecza do czasów
    nowożytnych (1226/1227–1835)', Archeologia Gdańska, 1 (2006),
    pp. 137–214
Murray, Alan, 'Contrasting Masculinities in the Baltic Crusades:
    Teutonic Knights and Secular Crusaders at War and Peace in
    Late Medieval Prussia', in Crusading and Masculinities, ed. Natasha
    Hodgson, Katherine Lewis and Matthew Mesley (London, 2019),
    pp. 113–28
Nicholson, Helen, 'The Role of Women in the Military Orders', Militiae
    Christi: Handelingen van de Vereniging voor de Studie over de Tempeliers
    en de Hospitaalridders vzw, 1 (2010), pp. 210–19.
Nowak, Zenon, 'Czy Prusy Krzyżackie były państwem nowożytnym?', in
    Architectura et historia, ed. Michał Woźniak (Toruń, 1999) pp. 79–89
Nowakowski, Andrzej, Arms and Armour in the Medieval Teutonic Order's
    State in Prussia (Łódź, 1994)
Ose, Ieva, 'Research on Medieval Castles in Latvia: Achievements and
    Problems", Kunstiteaduslikke Uurimusi, 25 (2016), pp. 23–42
—, 'Die Verwendung von Keramik in den Burgen Lettlands vom 13.–16.
    Jahrhundert', Castella Maris Baltici, 14 (2021), pp. 9–18
Palli, Heldur, Eesti rahvastiku ajalugu aastani 1712 (Tallinn, 1996), pp. 23
    and 40
Paravicini, Werner, Die Preußenreisen des europäischen Adels, 3 vols
    (Sigmaringen, 1989–95; repr. Göttingen, 2020)

Paszkiweicz, Borys, *Brakteaty – pieniądz średniowiecznych Prus* (Wrocław, 2009)

Phillips, Jonathan, *Holy Warriors: A Modern History of the Crusades* (New York, 2009)

Piirimäe, Pärtel, 'Staatenbund oder Ständestaat? Der livländische Landtag im Zeitalter Wolters von Plettenberg (1494–1535)', *Forschungen zur Baltischen Geschichte*, 8 (2013), pp. 40–80

Pluskowski, Aleksander, *The Archaeology of the Prussian Crusade: Holy War and Colonisation*, 2nd edn (London, 2022)

—, and Heiki Valk, 'The Archaeology of the Crusades in the Eastern Baltic', in *The Crusader World*, ed. Adrian Boas (London, 2015) pp. 568–92

—, et al., 'Late-Medieval Horse Remains at Cēsis Castle, Latvia, and the Teutonic Order's Equestrian Resources in Livonia', *Medieval Archaeology*, LXII/2 (2018), pp. 351–79

—, et al., 'Re-organizing the Livonian Landscape', in *Environment, Colonization, and the Baltic Crusader States*, ed. Aleksander Pluskowski (Turnhout, 2019), pp. 207–29

—, Heiki Valk, Juhan Kreem and Gundars Kalniŋš, 'Sites in Livonia: The Historical and Archaeological Background', in *Environment, Colonization, and the Baltic Crusader States*, ed. Aleksander Pluskowski (Turnhout, 2019), pp. 79–104

Poliński, Dariusz, *Pień: Siedziba krzyżackich prokuratorów w ziemi chełmińskiej* (Toruń, 2013)

—, 'Castrum Starkenberg w świetle najnowszych badań nad krzyżackimi obiektami obronnymi', in *życie społeczno-kulturalne w państwie Zakonu Krzyżackiego (XIII–XVI w.)*, ed. Jan Gancewski et al. (Olsztyn, 2016), pp. 7–24

Pósán, László, 'Prussian Missions and the Invitation of the Teutonic Order into Kulmerland', in *The North-Eastern Frontiers of Medieval Europe*, ed. Alan V. Murray (London, 2016), pp. 429–48

Pospieszny, Kazimierz, *Malborksa rezydencja wielkich mistrzów, królów i cesarzy* (Malbork, 1991)

—, 'Über den Gebrauch der Gebrannten erde zur Bildnerei: Warsztaty ceglarski i plastyka architektoniczna zamku w Malborku w XIII i XIV w', in *Cegła w architekturze środkowo-wschodniej Europy*, ed. Marian Arszyński and Mariusz Mierzwiński (Malbork, 2002), pp. 163–79

—, '1.2.13. Główny zwornik z "madonną tronującą" z kościoła zamkowego w Malborku, ok. 1340', in *Fundacje artystyczne na terenie Państwa Krzyżackiego w Prusach I*, ed. Barbara Pospieszna (Pelplin, 2010), pp. 35–6

Pringle, Denys, Andrew Petersen, M. Dow and C. Singer, 'Qal'at Jiddin:
    A Castle of the Crusader and Ottoman Periods in Galilee', *Levant*,
    26 (1994), pp. 135–66
Radzimiński, Andrzej, *Chrystianizacja i ewangelizacja Prusów: Historia i
    źródła* (Toruń, 2011)
Rowell, Stephen, *Lithuania Ascending: A Pagan Empire within East-
    Central Europe, 1295–1345* (Cambridge, 1994)
——, 'The Lithuano-Prussian Forest Frontier, c. 1422–1600', in *Frontiers in
    Question: Eurasian Borderlands, 700–1700*, ed. Daniel Power
    and Naomi Standen (Basingstoke, 1999), pp. 182–208
Rozynkowski, Waldemar, *Omnes Sancti et Sanctae Dei: Studium nad
    kultem świętych w diecezjach pruskich państwa zakonu krzyżackiego*
    (Malbork, 2006)
Rynkiewicz-Domino, Wiesława, '1.2.8. Segment fryzu z dekoracją
    maswerkową. ok. 1320', in *Fundacje artystyczne na terenie Państwa
    Krzyżackiego w Prusach*, ed. Barbara Pospieszna (Pelplin, 2010),
    p. 30
Sarnowsky, Jürgen, *Die Wirtschaftsführung des Deutschen Ordens in
    Preußen (1382–1454)* (Cologne, 1993)
——, *Der Deutsche Orden* (Munich, 2007)
Saunders, Corinne, *The Forest of Medieval Romance* (Cambridge, 1993)
Sawicki, Zbigniew, et al., 'Survival at the Frontier of Holy War:
    Political Expansion, Crusading, Environmental Exploitation
    and the Medieval Colonising Settlement at Biała Góra, North
    Poland', *European Journal of Archaeology*, XVIII/2 (2015),
    pp. 282–311
Schoenborn, Ulrich, 'Kurland im Horizont der Reformation: Resonanz –
    Korrelation – Interaktion', in *The Reformation in the Southeast Baltic
    Region*, ed. Arūnas Baublys and Vasilijus Safronovas (Klaipėda,
    2017), pp. 45–82
Seiler, Jörg, 'Daß der Teutsch Orden noch nit erloschen . . .: strukturelle
    Wandlungen des deutschen Ordens im Reich im Gefolge
    der Reformation', in *The Military Orders and the Reformation*,
    ed. Johannes A. Mol, Klaus Militzer and Helen J. Nicholson
    (Hilversum, 2006), pp. 139–80
Selart, Anti, *Livonia, Rus' and the Baltic Crusades in the Thirteenth
    Century* (Leiden, 2015)
Semiańczuk, Hienadź, 'Wiedza geograficzna w zakonie krzyżackim o
    ziemiach Białoruskich wielkiego Księstwa Litewskiego w XIV wieku',
    in *Kancelarie Krzyżackie: Stan badań i perspektywy badawcze*, ed.
    Janusz Trupinda (Malbork, 2002), pp. 225–34

Šnē, Andris, 'The Medieval Peasantry: On the Social and Religious Position of the Rural Natives in Southern Livonia (13th–15th Centuries)', *Ajalooline Ajakiri*, 1/2 (2008), pp. 89–100

—, 'The Early Town in Late Prehistoric Latvia', in *The Reception of Medieval Europe in the Baltic Sea Region*, ed. Jörn Staecker (Visby, 2009), pp. 127–36

Soczko, Adam, *Układy emporowe w architekturze państwa krzyżeackiego* (Warsaw, 2005)

Stephan, Joachim, 'Prusowie w gospodarstwie krzyżaków', in *Gospodarka ludów morza bałtyckiego starożytność i średniowiecze: Mare Integrans – Studia nad dziejami wybrzeży Morza Bałtyckiego*, ed. Michał Bogacki, Maciej Franz and Zbigniew Pilarczyk (Toruń, 2009), pp. 317–25

Šterns, Indriķis, *Latvijas vēsture, 1290–1500* (Riga, 1997)

Supruniuk, Anna, 'O wyprawach do Prus rycerczy polskich i wojnie domowej w koronie w latach 1382–1385', *Zapiski Historyczne*, 2 (2000), pp. 31–54

Tandecki, Janusz, 'Rozwój terytorialny państwa zakonnego w Prusach', in *Państwo zakonu krzyżackiego w Prusach: Władza i społeczeństwo*, ed. Marian Biskup et al. (Warsaw, 2009), pp. 105–9

—, 'Zakon krzyżacki', in *Państwo zakonu krzyżackiego w Prusach. Władza i społeczeństwo*, ed. Marian Biskup et al. (Warsaw, 2009), pp. 405–19

Țiplic, Ioan Marian, 'Cavalerii teutoni și fortificațiile lor din Țara Bârsei', *Corviniana*, 6 (2000), pp. 138–59

Toomaspoeg, Kristjan, 'Montfort Castle and the Order of the Teutonic Knights in the Latin East', in *Montfort: History, Early Research and Recent Studies of the Principal Fortress of the Teutonic Order in the Latin East*, ed. Adrian Boas and Rabei Khamisy (Leiden, 2017), pp. 15–23

Torbus, Tomas, *Die Konventsburgen im Deutschordensland Preussen* (Munich, 1998)

—, 'Communication between Centre and Periphery: The Example of the Italian Branch of the Teutonic Order (13th–16th Centuries)', *Ordines Militares*, 25 (2020), pp. 109–36

von Treitschke, Heinrich, 'Das deutsche Ordensland Preußen', *Preußische Jahrbücher*, 10 (1862), pp. 95–151

Trupinda, Janusz, '1.3.3. Zespół heraldyczny z herbem von Jungingen ok. 1400', in *Fundacje artystyczne na terenie Państwa Krzyżackiego w Prusach*, ed. Barbara Pospiezna (Pelplin, 2010), p. 85

Tvauri, Andres, 'Late Medieval Hypocausts with Heat Storage in Estonia', *Baltic Journal of Art History*, 1 (2009), pp. 49–78

Tyerman, Christopher, *God's War: A New History of the Crusades*
    (London, 2007)
Ubis, Edvinas, 'Archaeological Data as Evidence of Cultural Interaction
    between the Teutonic Order and Local Communities: Problems and
    Perspectives', *Archaeologia Baltica*, 25 (2018), pp. 164–76
Urban, William, *The Teutonic Knights: A Military History* (London,
    2003)
——, *The Last Years of the Teutonic Knights: Lithuania, Poland and the
    Teutonic Order* (Barnsley, 2019)
Valk, Heiki, et al., 'Thirteenth Century Cultural Deposits at the Castle
    of the Teutonic Order in Karksi', *Arheoloogilised välitööd Eestis/
    Archaeological Field Work in Estonia 2012* (Tallinn, 2013), pp. 73–92
    (Estonian and English)
Veldi, Martti, 'Roads and Hill Forts in Southern Estonia during the
    German Conquest in Henry's *Chronicle of Livonia*', in *Strongholds and
    Power Centres East of the Baltic Sea in the 11th–13th Centuries*, ed.
    Heiki Valk (Tartu, 2014), pp. 385–416
Wasik, Bogusz, 'Parchamy z zamków Krzyżackich – technika budowy i
    zabudowa', *Komunikaty Mazursko-Warmińskie*, 11/288 (2015),
    pp. 269–80
——, 'Budownictwo i architektura zamków krzyzackich w Prusach', in
    Sapientia aedificavit sibi domum, ed. Janusz Trupinda (Malbork, 2019),
    pp. 364–83
Wenskus, Reinhard, 'Das Ordensland Preußen als Territorialstaat des 14.
    Jahrhunderts', in *Der deutsche Territorialstaat im 14. Jahrhundert*, ed.
    Hans Patze, vol. 1 (Frankfurt am Main, 1970), pp. 347–82
Wiewióra, Marcin, 'Długi wiek XIII – początki krzyżackiej murowanej
    architektury obronnej na ziemi chełmińskiej w świetle najnowszych
    badan', *Archaeologia Historica Polona*, 22 (2014), pp. 113–44
——, 'Gród i zamek w państwie krzyżackim – miejsce tradycji czy tradycja
    miejsca?', *Archaeologia Historica Polona*, 24 (2016), pp. 195–231
——, 'Najstarsze fazy osadnictwa krzyżackiego na zamkach w Unisławiu,
    Zamku Bierzgłowskim i Starogrodzie: Studia nad osadnictwem
    obronnym na ziemi chełmińskiej w XIII wieku', *Archaeologia Historica
    Polona*, 26 (2018), pp. 239–64
Wihoda, Martin, 'The Premyslid Dynasty and the Teutonic Order', in
    The Crusades and the Military Orders, ed. Zsolt Hunyadi and József
    Laszlovszky (Budapest, 2001), pp. 337–47
Woziński, Andrzej, 'Późnogotycka rzeźba w państwie zakonnym', in
    Fundacje artystyczne na terenie Państwa Krzyżackiego w Prusach II,
    ed. Barbara Pospieszna (Pelplin, 2010), pp. 195–212

Zimmermann, Harald, *Der Deutsche Orden im Burzenland: Eine diplomatische Untersuchung* (Cologne, 2000)

Žulkus, Vladas, 'Der Hausbau in Klaipėda (Memel)', in *Lübecker Kolloquium zur Stadtarchäologie im Hanseraum III: der Hausbau*, ed. Brigitte Dahmen et al. (Lübeck, 2001), pp. 529–49

—, 'Die mittelalterliche und frühneuzeitliche Infrastuktur der Stadt Memel', in *Lübecker Kolloquium zur Stadtarchäologie im Hanseraum IV: die Infrastruktur*, ed. Regina Dunckel et al. (Lübeck, 2004), pp. 371–84

ACKNOWLEDGEMENTS

The author and publishers would like to thank Dr Eva Eihmane for her comments on this book during its preparation.

Photo Acknowledgements

The author and publishers wish to express their thanks to the sources listed below for illustrative material and/or permission to reproduce it. Some locations of artworks are also given below, in the interest of brevity:

Central Archives of Historical Records, Warsaw (Parchment Documents Collection, ref. 1062): p. 140; courtesy Peter Dennis: p. 116; photos courtesy Magnus Elander: pp. 63, 97, 128 (re-enactment Łukasz Dutkiewicz); from Christoph Hartknoch, *Alt- und Neues Preussen oder Preussischer Historien zwey Theile* (Frankfurt and Leipzig, 1684), photo Staatsbibliothek zu Berlin: p. 115; photo courtesy Christofer Herrmann: p. 144; Herzog Anton Ulrich-Museum, Braunschweig: p. 159; photo courtesy Rabei G. Khamisy: p. 34; courtesy Marta Lielbriede: p. 166; courtesy Paweł Moszczyński: pp. 100, 123, 127; Old Town Hall (Ratusz Staromiejski), Toruń: pp. 58–9; maps Aleksander Pluskowski: pp. 10, 61, 81 (after Marian Biskup et al., eds, *Państwo zakonu krzyżackiego w Prusach: Władza i społeczeństwo* (Warsaw, 2009); after Dariusz Poliński, *Późnośredniowieczne osadnictwo wiejskie w ziemi chełmińskiej* (Toruń, 2003); and after Friedrich Benninghoven, 'Probleme der Zahl und Standort-verteilung der livländischen Streitkräfte im ausgehenden Mittelalter', in *Zeitschrift für Ostforschung*, XII (1963)), 82 and 101 (both after Biskup et al., 2009), 148 (after Benninghoven, 1963); photos Aleksander Pluskowski: pp. 35, 40, 46, 47, 71, 102–3, 108, 146; private collection: pp. 91, 151; photo courtesy Zbyszek Sawicki: p. 62; from C. Steinbrecht, *Die Baukunst des deutschen Ritterordens in Preussen*, vol. III: *Schloss Lochstedt und seine Malereien* (Berlin, 1910), photo National Library (Biblioteka Narodowa), Warsaw: p. 111; Stiftsbibliothek, St Gallen (Cod. Sang. 1084, p. 47): p. 106; Universitätsbibliothek Heidelberg (Cod. Pal. germ. 848, fol. 264r): p. 17; Wikimedia Commons: pp. 28 (photo Tilman2007, CC BY-SA 4.0), 98 (photo Monika Towiańska, CC BY-SA 4.0), 109 (photo Dawid Galus, CC BY-SA 3.0 PL).

INDEX

Page numbers in *italics* refer to illustrations